D1486605

*An Essay
on the Theory of
Enlightened
Despotism*

An Essay on the Theory of Enlightened Despotism

Leonard Krieger

The University of Chicago Press
Chicago and London

Leonard Krieger is University Professor of History at the University of Chicago.
He is the author of several books, including *The German Idea of Freedom* and
The Politics of Discretion.

The University of Chicago Press, Chicago 60637
The University of Chicago Press, Ltd., London

Library of Congress Cataloging in Publication Data
Krieger, Leonard.
  An essay on the theory of enlightened despotism.
  Bibliography: p.
  Includes index.
  1. Despotism — History. 2. Political science —
History. 3. Enlightenment. 4. Europe — Politics and
government — 18th century. I. Title.
JC381.K8 321.6 74-16684
ISBN 0-226-45299-9

Contents

To Alan, David, and Nathaniel—enlightened citizens

Preface

As every collegian and graduate student and every teacher of collegians and graduate students knows, there is a radical difference of conception between a term paper and a seminar paper, and radically different standards of composition and of evaluation must be applied to each genre. In the first, a position is taken or an interpretation hypothesized, and adequate evidence is mustered — measuring adequacy by both sufficiency and cogency — to make the case or sustain the interpretation; disputes may arise about the quality of the selection but plenitude is not a relevant criterion. In the second (the seminar paper), a topic is plumbed for all the available evidence pertinent to it in order to transmit as complete a representation of the topic as possible, with any ultimate position or interpretation emerging from the composition of the material.

The distinction holds despite the protestations of purists that: (*a*) the plenitude of available evidence must be known before adequate selection can be made; (*b*) there must and should always be some selection of evidence even in the most complete of inquiries; and (c) positions and interpretations always guide as well as predicate the collection and presentation of the evidence which supports them. The distinction holds because it is based on the logic of scholarship rather than, like the protestations, on its psychology — that is, the distinction has to do not with the way scholars actually operate on their material and their conclusions but with the rules by which they test their results, and good pedagogy has required the acknowledgment of, and training in, at least these two sets of rules and their derivative respective procedures.

These genres, which are thus formally and overtly differentiated in educational exercises, naturally tend to overlap in professional practice, but nonetheless this same intentional distinction does extend to scholarly publications of both articular and volumed dimensions. The confusion of these genres, indeed, ranks high among the conditions which produce the bewildering incongruities in the judgment of academic performance and the frustrating occasions for authors and reviewers to argue past each other. The "essay" and the "monograph" may stand as the professional terminological equivalents of the accepted tutorial forms, so long as it is understood from the parallel that in this context an essay does mean something more academically serious — that is, evidentially grounded — and a monograph may mean something less necessarily unidimensional than these expressions generally connote.

Let it be clear, then, that what follows is an essay in this academic sense. It is an attempt to see what the historical phenomenon which has been covered by the label "enlightened despotism" looks like when it is viewed, in accordance with our changed perspectives on the recently disarranged eighteenth century and on our own dubious political arrangements, as a pocket of coherence in an acknowledged manifold of human circumstance rather than from the traditional angle as a political system manqué. To clarify through a mechanical analogy so dear to our own culture, it is time to look at enlightened despotism rather as *a* thread through a maze than *the* magnet which organizes all the surrounding particles in accordance with its own field of force and whose strength or weakness is measured by the span and regularity of its lawful symmetry.

Such a shift of perspective alters the historical status of enlightened despotism in three ways. First, from being the distinctive and dominant political system of an era it becomes one of several attempts at resolving newly exacerbated social divisions. Second, from measurement by standards of assessment based upon the logicality of its theory and the literal extent of its contemporary endorsement the dimensions of enlightened despotism now get gauged for their representative capacity by the qualitative fidelity with which they reflect the otherwise uncrystallized and unmeasurable intersections of tradition and innovation in the society, however inconsistent the combination and whatever the quantitative calculation of its actual adoption in the eighteenth century. And finally, from the status of a rhetorical flourish upon a checkered practice the theory of enlightened despotism achieves a new historiographical value as the arena in which, through the perceptible modulation of ideas, the interaction of tradition and innovation becomes most intelligible. Under this new dispensation it seems more desirable to see what enlightened despotism looks like by analyzing its intellectual structure without the criterion of an ideal type of theoretical absolutism, against the background of inherited monarchical doctrine, and through the selection of specimens for the transparency of their reconciled contradictions, than to make still another attempt at resolving the historiographical dispute about its importance for the eighteenth century by making an exhaustive survey of its effects.

Enlightened despotism, moreover, gets to be more than a purely historical problem when it is viewed as a comparatively credible recourse against confusion rather than as a dubious and evanescent stage in the history of autocracy. For who will deny that periodically, down to and including our very own day, men have submitted themselves to a political power bound only by the discretion of the rulers who exercise it and that men continue to submit to such power whenever, confused and divided about their own interests and values, they attribute to rulers, precisely because of their position as rulers, the information and wisdom that transforms the old adage, "knowledge is power," from an ambivalent description of actuality to a perilous principle of authoritarian morality? The fact is that enlightened despotism has survived the institution of monarchy, on which it first battened, to become a permanent category, a continual option, and a recurrent choice in our politics. On the infrequent occasions when we do acknowledge it we tend to justify it as a temporary expedient or a particular dependence which may well represent an aberration from political principle but to which no political principle of its own attaches. This view of enlightened despotism has found support in the critical historical interpretation which has depreciated its validity in similar terms for the eighteenth century, but now, with the rise of our suspicion that an unacknowledged principle may indeed underlie so many reversions to enlightened despots, however euphemistic their modern titles and exceptional the emergencies, we can take a fresh look at the eighteenth century for elucidation of *this* problem — that is, for more light on how principles get adjusted to deal with situations which exceed their grasp.

From this point of view the eighteenth-century theorists of enlightened despotism became especially useful because, isolated and unrepresentative as the *fact* of their theoretical advocacy may have been, the *manner* of it affords an articulate clue to the process of accommodation which remained sporadic and inarticulate both in their contemporaries and in ours. Since the substance of their theoretical achievement, in adapting the pervasive institutional orderliness of seventeenth-century political organisms, was to detach absolutism from traditional monarchy and to make it a versatile schema, available to all kinds of political regimes, the "what" as well as the "how" of their performance is obviously of far more than antiquarian interest. The recent caricatures of historical relevance, with their requirements of a one-to-one correlation between the events of the past and the issues of the present, may well be out of style, but the abiding relevance of history remains: it restores our consciousness of those things in our lives which have sunk beneath the level of consciousness. Here, beyond the problems and polemics of acadmic history, is the raison d'être of this essay.

Anyone who has published knows the inadequacy of the prefatory format for the acknowledgment of debt and the expression of gratitude, but I hope that those to whom I here address it will understand the genuineness of the appreciation under the mask of the familiar ritual. First, I must once more pay public tribute to my wife, who, to this as to everything else that I have done, has applied both the inimitable intellectual precision that clarifies, rectifies, and identifies ideas and the sympathetic consideration that makes criticism constructive. Then I owe to Hanna Gray the programmatic occasion of an American Historical Association meeting and to Emile Karaffiol the balanced paper on enlightened despotism from which my rethinking of the theory took its start. Marc Raeff and Orest Ranum listened to my pilot paper on the theme and, with their usual perceptiveness, asked the kind of pertinent and provocative questions that spurred my development of it. Finally, I am much beholden to my colleague William H. McNeill for the encouragement without which I am not at all sure that I should have proceeded to the publication of this modest effort.

Portions of the Introduction are reprinted, with permission, from Leonard Krieger, "The Distortions of Political Theory: The XVIIth Century Case," *Journal of the History of Ideas* 25 (1964): 325–31.

Introduction

The Seventeenth-Century Model

Our political thinking revolves around the ideas of freedom and power, and our political thinkers seek orbits that connect these ideas rationally with each other and organically with fundamental principles of anthropology and morality. The ideas, in their recognizable political form, we have received from the sixteenth and the eighteenth centuries; the models of the linkages, both internal and external, from the seventeenth and the nineteenth. Whether the difference in vintage between the ideas and their contexts contributes to confusion in our own politics is difficult for us to judge contemporaneously, but it is clear that the difference has led to problems in the historical judgment of eighteenth-century politics. Its ideas of freedom and power appear to be sandwiched between architectonic eras in our retrospection, and if we can illuminate the historical problem we may get a clue to the resolution of our own.

In general, we have come far in disentangling the interpolations of the nineteenth century from the contributions of the eighteenth, but we have not done nearly so well in following the transmutation of the seventeenth century's well-ordered postulates during the eighteenth; and to this extent (with due apologies to Whitehead), we fall victim to what we may call the fallacy of misplaced completeness. Our limitations in this respect are due to something more essential than the occupational imbalance of historians, who can easily identify anachronisms that have been projected backward in time but do not so readily detect those that under color of psychic and social inertia are protruded forward in time. The explanation entails something more substantial, too, than the bits and pieces of mooring which any idea carries with it when it is translated from one era to another.

The primary reason for our difficulty in ascertaining the distinctive character of eighteenth-century political thinking vis-à-vis seventeenth lies in the historical fact that when eighteenth-century publicists took up the themes of political power and personal rights from the systematic format in which Grotius, Hobbes, Pufendorf, and Locke had transmitted these themes, they deliberately included such structural concomitants as the concepts of natural law, social contract, and sovereignty — not inadvertently, but because they needed these linkages for their own purposes. Hence the deceptive appearance of filiation, and hence too the apparent similarity in the standards of consistency to be applied to the two generations of political ideas. Eighteenth-century political theory has seemed to depart from its seventeenth-century forebear merely in the greater flexibility of its logical junctures, in its preference for the assumption rather than the exposition of primary principles, and in the more mobile grace of its rhetoric. But actually the context and the function of its linkages were radically different from those of the great seventeenth-century systems, and so are the categories of understanding which hold for it. The assertion of this change in context, and the analysis of this change in function, constitute the theme of the following chapters. Here it will suffice to indicate the *terminus a quo* of the process, the seventeenth-century orientation that furnished the original setting of the eighteenth-century ideas, their terms of reference, and, perhaps inevitably, the grounds for their misunderstanding.

The decisive feature of seventeenth-century political theorizing, for our purpose, was the close association between the systematic form of its doctrines and the rational structure it predicated as the essential substance of political reality. The most prominent (or notorious) bearers of this theorizing to the next century — Grotius, Hobbes, Spinoza, Pufendorf, Locke — were at least as committed to the exposition of primary principles in a highly stratified philosophy, theology, jurisprudence, or in any combination thereof as they were to the analysis of political society; and if the precise ratio of autonomy to dependence in the relationship of politics as such to the prior system is moot for each case, there is clearly a continuity of specific architectonic ideas through which the organizing concepts from the more general levels of reality become the pillars of an a priori order in politics.

For each of the great seventeenth-century theorists, indeed, the foundations of political society are beset with confusion and even antinomy until a suprapolitical framework is invoked to supply the connecting assumptions. Thus Grotius, whose historical fame rests on his formal dissociation of natural-law politics from theology, could only sustain his conservative conviction that the "source" of this intellectually detached law was the "maintenance of the social order" by restoring its connection with "the free will of God to which beyond all cavil our reason tells us we must render obedience."[1] Hobbes went so far in the direction of emancipating the rules of politics nominally from prior sanctions as to deny the validity of "the notions of Right and Wrong, Justice and Injustice," and consequently of law as such, before the establishment of political community, and he thereby posed the apparent problem for which he has been notorious — the assertion of a political obligation that transcends the self-preserving motive that is its ground. But it is only a seeming contradiction that has been readily resolved by uncovering the substratal relevance to Hobbes's politics of his Christian eschatology, of his adherence to the natural-law tradition with its built-in prescriptive connotations, and of the "unity of the Hobbesian philosophy" that patterns the "artificial man" — that is, the state—on the organic and ethical model of the natural man.[2]

If Hobbes was the most influential—even if only by the standards required for refutation[3]—of the radical systemizers in seventeenth-century political theory, he does not represent their extreme. Less infamous for his politics to his contemporaries than was Hobbes, Spinoza yet manifests to us such an unqualified version of apparent political antinomy and such a compensatory wholeness of authoritative ontological harmony that he reveals even more decisively than Hobbes the organized view of fundamental reality that underlay seventeenth-century rationalism. In one and the same context—his discussion of the ideal state—Spinoza maintained all four of two opposing sets of principles, holding that human rights were defined both by power and by reason and declaring with equal ambiguity that individuals were both the sovereign possessors of freedom and the total subjects of an unlimited sovereign authority. Thus on the one hand he could apparently combine naturalism and individualism by asserting that according to the "sovereign law and right of nature ... each individual should endeavor to preserve itself as it is, without regard to anything but itself"; that therefore "my natural right is ... co-extensive with my power" and "a compact is only made valid by its utility"; and that, as applied to government, the principle that sovereign right is defined by the possession of sovereign power means that the ruler will retain "such sovereign right ... only so long as he maintains the power of enforcing his will."

On the other hand, Spinoza could with equal plausibility combine rationalism and authoritarianism by asserting that "the more a man is guided by reason, the more he is free, the more constantly he will keep the laws of the commonwealth, and execute the commands of the supreme authority, whose subject he is." The paradoxical result of these superficially ill-assorted principles was Spinoza's advocacy of democracy, as the form of government which is "the most consonant with individual liberty"—and yet in which "every citizen depends not on himself but on the commonwealth, all whose commands he is bound to execute ...; what the state decides to be just and good must be held to be so decided by every individual," so that "however iniquitous the subject may think the commonwealth's decisions, he is nonetheless bound to execute them." But neither the principles nor the results were paradoxical for Spinoza, for behind this politics lay the metaphysical structure of his *Ethics*, which identified the congruent right and power of individuals in nature with the unitary right and power of God and which, through the divine articulation, presumed for every natural right participation in the "eternal order of nature," for "according to the necessity of this order only are all individual beings determined in a fixed manner to exist and operate."[4]

Pufendorf and Locke furnish the limiting cases for the rational ordering of the political world. Both represented the intellectual generation spawned by the later decades of the seventeenth century through their larger susceptibility—vis-à-vis their forebears—to the empirical manifold of human behavior, in their politics and even in their consideration of the more schematized realms of theology, philosophy, and jurisprudence outside it. And yet in these figures too the few principles of composition which they did advance exercised an authoritative dominion over the concrete multiplicity of things; and if they no longer subscribed to the definite hierarchy of knowledge which once guaranteed the affiliation of political categories with the propositions of the more rigorous sciences, they did define transitional arenas in which the synthetic principles of their theology, philosophy, or law took politicizable forms.

Pufendorf outgrew his early addiction to the Cartesian deductive methods, but in his politics and history as well as in his later jurisprudence and theology he continued to seek out the cardinal principles from which the demonstrable truth in all fields would necessarily follow. Again, he came to place great store in the autonomy of each of these fields, both as a discipline of knowledge and as a realm of men's social life, but the centrality which he accorded to the distinctive arena of the "state of nature," as the intersection of the constituent order and the discretionary vagaries of human existence, was an exemplary indication of the structural connections between his ethics and jurisprudence on the one hand and his politics on the other.[5] Small wonder that he found irregularity of political forms "monstrous" and intolerable in his discussion of the German Empire.[6]

In Locke, finally, we have the progenitor of eighteenth-century thought whose work in the substratal fields of philosophy (empiricism) and theology (deism), as well as in the practical field of politics (constitutionalism), could be applied with least adaptation to the appreciation of tangible and variable worldly concerns. Much has been made of the distance between Locke and his earlier seventeenth-century antecedents, both in his separation of the fields of his thinking (especially anent the inapplicability of sensationalism in the epistemology of the *Essay on Human Understanding* to the prescription of the general natural law of the *Two Treatises of Government*) and in the casual irresolution of the palpable inconsistencies within each of the fields of his thinking (especially between the epistemology and the ethics in the *Essay* and between the general rationality and specific irrationality of men in the *Two Treatises*). Undoubtedly in these respects Locke took a considerable step toward the looser methods and the slacker logical standards which would characterize the eighteenth-century turn of mind. But the same vintage of recent commentaries that has stressed the diversity and fragmentation of eighteenth-century thinking has tended to seek the reconstruction of integrity in Locke. The assumption is that whether the substantive synthetic factor is to be found in traditional natural-law atavisms or in novel individualistic doctrines there was in Locke an underlying formal continuity, of indefinite attitude or identifiable principle, that aligns him with the century of his birth and development. This hypothetical continuity of attitude is supported by the parallelism in Locke's endeavors, within each of the fields of his concern, to spread a rational net over a recalcitrant existence, and by his reiterated tendency to invoke religion as an aid to fallible reason in the crucial enterprises of understanding and controlling reality as a whole. For the continuity of logical structure, reference has been made — significantly for the seventeenth-century association — to the philosophical "hedonistic anthropology" of the *Essay on Human Understanding*. where Locke's analysis of human nature putatively furnishes the mechanism for the implicit connection between the descriptive vagaries of independent individuals and the prescriptive uniformity of the classic natural law in his politics.[7] If historiography mirrors history with any fidelity at all, Locke's political theory was dominated by the ideal of a pervasive rational order that was all the more emphatic in principle for its attenuation in substance. The incessant noting of inconsistencies by Lockean scholars is a function of the pervasive standard of rationality raised by Locke himself.

The force of a logically integrated system can be measured by the result of its encounter with resistant facts, whether in the formulation, the elaboration, or the testing of its design. The force varies directly with the distortion of the facts and inversely with the deflection of the system.[8] The seventeenth-century intellectual systems that interest us here are those which expound the nature, origins, and extent of the state (used here in its broadest sense to include the British preference for "civil society" or "commonwealth"). We may assess the presumption of logicality in the seventeenth-century political system by considering three sample doctrines, taken from their most formal proponents, which were molded in the engagement of formative principles with contemporary experience. International law, sovereignty, and toleration: in these doctrines real experiences which expanded the actual dominion of political power were conceived theoretically as so many limits upon political power. Hence they furnish appropriate gauges for calculating the respective force of the concept and the fact; and they furnish too appropriate media for understanding how the dominant force, in these cases the logic of the concepts, engages the heterogeneous category of the facts in sufficiently homologous terms to absorb the facts and distort them.

In their most systematic format the contraposition of such doctrines to the perceptible political circumstances of their formulation — a contraposition which is the necessary precondition of our inquiry—is dramatically manifest. Grotius set forth the existence of a secular law of nations, grounded in the absolute prescriptions of natural law and extended by consensus, which conferred real obligations as well as rights upon the heads of states in the initiation of war and in its conduct, as well as in peace, at a time when the states of Europe were administering a naked *raison d'état* in their bellicose relations, qualified only by the religious passion which was the one modification that Grotius categorically excluded. Hobbes recognized the reality of all states worthy of the name to consist in the exercise of an absolute, indivisible, and inalienable sovereignty resting only on the consent of the governed in exchange for the rendition of a well-defined set of security services to the governed, at a time when throughout Europe princes were still being widely regarded as the anointed of God; when they were justifying this regard with their sectarian meddling and their self-image of the Christian patriarch; when aristocracies were still fighting for a divided sovereignty; and when, in his own England, these actual confusions of politics were culminating in a bloody civil war. Locke's generally "non-historical theory of politics" has been attributed to his ultimate reliance upon "principles of nature and reason which lie outside of history and do not change with its changes," and to which, consequently, at least this kind of factuality does not appear "relevant."[9] Consistently with such principles, he argued in the special context of politics and religion that, since political power "is bounded and confined to the only care of promoting" the "civil interests" of the community and since a church is "a free and voluntary society" for public worship effectual to the salvation of the souls of its constituents, toleration as a principle is a necessary consequence of the very nature of both state and church.[10] But he argued this at a time when Louis XIV was revoking the permissive Edict of Nantes, the Stuarts were employing toleration as a sectarian instrument, and the grudging concessions of the subsequent revolutionary settlement made toleration smack more of political necessity than of either political or religious principle.

But when these relations are so summarized we seem to have overshot our mark. Each theorist seems to be not so much distorting political reality as rejecting it. The thesis of rejection would, moreover, appear to be confirmed by the support of empirical evidence. Thus Grotius explicitly announced in 1625 that he wrote his masterwork, *On the Law of War and Peace*, as a protest against the contemporary practice of international relations: "Throughout the Christian world I observed a lack of restraint in relation to war, such as even barbarous nations would be ashamed of."[11] In the same vein Locke expressed, during 1689, the publication year of his famous first *Letter on Toleration*, his dissatisfaction with the concessionary Toleration Act.[12] The implications of this evidence for our problem are serious indeed. It would sustain the obvious thesis that the differential factor between a political theory and a straight description or analysis of political reality is the normative element in the former—that the gap between the distortion and the rejection of political reality is merely a matter of degree and that both may be corrected simply by measuring the strength and deviation of unrealized ideals. Were this so, little more would need to be said and the historian could claim no special function in the business save perhaps to document the discrepancies. But, for seventeenth-century theory at least, this is not quite so.

To counter the outer buttress of specific confirming evidence first, we find that the repulsion of both Grotius and Locke from contemporary practice is germane to their *publication* of the works in question rather than to the ideas which they embody. Grotius had worked out the essence of his principles on international law in his unpublished *Law of Prizes* of 1604, and this on the occasion of confirming rather than repudiating a contemporary practice. Locke wrote his *Letter on Toleration* during 1685 and 1686, before the Revolution, but, more significantly, his basic theory of the subject goes back to his unpublished *Essay on Toleration* of 1667, when, far from the discordance of reality from his ideals, he was just beginning to work out the political theory of those ideals under the stimulus of the practical politics which he found in Shaftesbury's household.[13] As for Hobbes, the easy conclusion which might be drawn from the coincidence of his political phase with the revolutionary turmoil that he abhorred should be qualified by his judicious statement in the conclusion of the *Leviathan* that he had shown when and why men were politically obligated to a conqueror because "the civil wars have not yet sufficiently taught men" these truths and that, although "occasioned by the disorders of the present time," his work had no other design than "without partiality . . . to set before men's eyes the mutual relation between protection and obedience."[14]

So much for the neutralization of the bits and pieces. The main point supporting the position that the distortion of political reality by the natural-law theorists was something more fundamental and more interesting than its present rejection and future reformation in terms of a norm was the basic conviction, common to the whole school, that, far from being an ideal as yet unrealized, their norm was itself already a reality. It can be maintained, of course, that whatever their conviction they actually put into this reality what they wanted to see it become and that it is still essentially a case of the ideal versus the real. But to argue this is to commit the genetic fallacy. It is important, certainly, for the understanding of any principle, to identify whatever normative component there may be in it, but when this principle is conceived by its author as a constituent of reality, then its validity and its meaning depend upon its function as a constituent of reality. The tendency of recent scholarship to divest Hobbes and Locke of ethical or epistemological apriorism in approaching their political theory reinforces this position. Macpherson starts "by assuming that Hobbes was trying to do what he said he was doing, i.e. deducing political obligation from the supposed or observed facts of man's nature," and he maintains, moreover, that Hobbes's theory of this nature was accurate and adequate "as a reflection of his insight into the behavior of men toward each other" in the society of his time.[15] Laslett insists on the autonomy of Locke's political theory from his philosophy, shows its growth in the context of practical politics, and maintains that for Locke the rational natural law "at all points . . . must be compared with, made to fit into, the observed, the empirical facts about the created world and human behavior."[16] Grotius needs no such secondary support, for he himself supplemented his well-known dictum divorcing the validity of natural law from the authority of God with the explicit foundation of it upon the actuality of men's "strong bent toward social life."[17]

If, then, we accept the theorists' claim that for them the natural law which was their norm was descriptive of reality and had been discovered by them in reality, the question follows: what kind of reality, and how does it square with the unmistakable reality of the contemporary conditions that were antithetical to it? Their answer in essence was: it is a *general* kind of reality, and it is related to contemporary conditions as the universal and unitary is to the particular and diverse. The most rhetorical expression of this position is Hobbes's characterization of his *Leviathan* as a model of self-knowledge in the sense of knowing "not this, or that particular man, but Mankind," since the thoughts and passions of men are similar but their objects vary, and it is in connection with this variation that "the dissembling, lying, counterfeiting, and erroneous doctrines" enter which obscure truth.[18] More common to the school was the philosophical formulation which derived the "existence" of natural law from the universal qualities of man's real nature and made it the norm of human relations in the sense of its representing the dimension of human reality that was unified and therefore meaningful. Thus Grotius equated "the law of nature" with "the nature of man," and he accepted as proofs of this law both the logical consequence of man's "rational and social nature" and the existent general consensus of men on the rules of human relations.[19] For the whole school, the state of nature was a device to demonstrate men's universal qualities, in terms of which the laws of nature were both descriptive and prescriptive, prior to social differentiation. Whether or not the state of nature has ever existed as the integral human condition, the natural-law theorists were agreed that it has always existed and still exists on the level of what is common within and among all men. It underlay Locke's political theory and it underlay too his doctrine of toleration: "The sum of all we drive at is that every man may enjoy the same rights that are granted to others."[20] Toleration was not to Locke a specific concession or a blessing of variety: it was a real universal right to voluntary worship which was obscured by the particular varieties of intolerance.

Let us grant the theorists' version of their own procedure: the general qualities of human nature and behavior are known to be real because they are derived from the observation, comparison, and analysis of the particular facts of individuals and societies in history and contemporary life, without which general qualities this history and this life become incomprehensible. The natural laws which make a norm of these general qualities for particular human activities are known to be real because they simply translate the qualities into men's relations with one another: they express, that is, what is common to the various types of human relations; they are what would later be called concrete universals, generalities that have real existence. Thus there are two levels of reality, doubly related: on one, the general level is known from the particular level; on the other, men integrate themselves by approaching what they do in particular in accordance with what they are in general.

If we grant that the theorists were indeed doing this, then any distortion between their general theory and the particular political reality around them becomes explicable: they make general and categorical propositions out of what in particular practice is graded and shaded. Grotius made secular international law out of the actual tendency, hybrid as it was, of the European nations to form a system of states, each a sovereign unit and related to others by the communicable formulation of their long-range, intersecting interests which was implemented through permanent diplomatic institutions for negotiating the intersections. Hobbes's doctrine of sovereignty registered the actual tendency, equally adulterated and obscured by the spectacular division and conflict of religions, of central governments to absorb the authority of churches and nobles not merely through the vacillating fortunes of conflict but more importantly through the increased services to the regional community that the central power was able to render. Locke's notion of toleration, finally, full as it was of the traditional ideas which for a century and a half had been crying in the wilderness for the Christian charity, the fideistic otherworldliness and the nonsectarian practical ethic of the Gospel, developed into a full-blown and memorable theory when he generalized from the increasing actual tendency of governments to define their religious functions by their political needs. Locke thereby provided the basis for his dictum that "whatsoever is lawful in the commonwealth cannot be prohibited by the magistrate in the church."[21] We may identify the distortion, then, as the degree by which the general propositions of the theory, conditioned as they are by the universal and logical requirements of reason, deviate from the observable sum of actual particulars.

It behooves us now to assess the converse of the relationship — that is, the deflection of the system — by considering the primary theories for undue emphases, inconsistencies, qualifications, and complications which betray the impact of positive facts that could not be integrated into the logic of the system. Thus Grotius's well-known addiction to the authority of Scripture, positive law, and its commentators; his cloudy notion of sovereignty; the use of the doctrine of consent to cover the problematic relationship between the rules of international law prescribed by the law of nature and the usually more permissive provisions of the "voluntary" or customary law of nations: all these manifest Grotius's wrestling with particular realities that did not entirely fit into his rational scheme. Hobbes's system is much tighter and consequently less susceptible to this kind of analysis. It is quite definitely not appropriate to such fundamental issues as the relations of his philosophy and his politics or the moral source of his political obligation, but it may well be applicable to his overly protested concern with religion in general and Catholicism in particular. Locke is more systematic in his religious liberalism than in other sections of his theory which have been called into question, but in his inability to decide, by virtue of his principles, the crucial issue of a conflict between the prescription of a sovereign and the conscience of the individual in matters of morals which relate both to civil interests and to salvation, and in his exclusion of atheists, Mohammedans, and implicitly Roman Catholics from the orbit of toleration, there may be seen evidence not only of his own latitudinarian Protestantism but also of an attempt to come to terms with contemporary practice.

A second way to assess the deflection of system is to investigate secondary theorists — disciples, adapters, popularizers. These second-level figures tend to be less rigorous in their logic and more open to particular influences of the environment than their mentors. Consequently they exhibit a diminished angle of factual distortion and an increased — and more visible — angle of theoretical deflection. Hence they show how the general propositions of theory can be modulated or opened up so as to account more precisely for the existing balance of particular movements and institutions. Pufendorf, one of the most-read theorists of the century, may double for Grotius and Hobbes, whom he sought to combine, in this function.[22] He adapted Grotius to contemporary international relations by limiting the binding force of international law to the prescription of rational grounds for starting war and frankly reducing all other aspects of international affairs in war and peace to the will of the sovereign who is bound only by the interests of his own state. He adapted Hobbes to contemporary political practice and operational beliefs by reintroducing God as the necessary if indirect source of political obligation; by applying the concept of sovereignty indiscriminately and without favor to all unmixed forms of the state, including tortuously therein even the species of "limited sovereignties"; and by accommodating the concept to the idea of a politically subordinate corporate society, of a kind that did prevail in Europe. For

Locke, we may adduce the figure of Christian Thomasius, who crossed Locke with Pufendorf to incubate a doctrine of toleration based upon the moral purpose of sovereign policy. If we move from Locke to Thomasius to Christian Wolff, who extended the sovereign's rights over the realm of the spirit, to Frederick the Great and his policy of toleration grounded in religious indifference, civic ethics, and political expediency, a full circle is achieved: the general principle which was drawn from particular politics and transcended it is brought back down, with suitable modification, into it.[23]

But with the closing of this circle we have reached the point at which differences of degree have graduated into a difference of kind. At some indeterminable point during the first half of the eighteenth century the inconsistencies and incongruities of theory which betokened the intellectual awareness of exceptional and indigestible facts became a part of the rule, justified by the flexibility of reason in accounting for the rich variety of human existence. By the second half of the century the relationship of fact and system had become reversed: factual distortion was deliberately reduced, and by the same measure theoretical deflection graduated into distortion. Whereas seventeenth-century theorists strove everywhere for consistency and distorted facts in the service of their conceptual logic, the publicists of the later eighteenth century accepted conflict and diversity and did not hesitate to distort the logic of their theory to cover the variegated clusters of their social facts. They could distort political logic and yet have it serve the function of accountability only by adapting the synthetic concepts of their more systematic antecedents to the newer circumstantial emphasis. The change in the parameters of theoretical endeavor and the consequent modulation of crucial political concepts — developments which jointly made a theory of enlightened despotism conceivable and, in a schematic way, characteristic — are the themes of the following chapters.

Absolutism and Despotism 1

Enlightened despotism has had a very bad press of late. The possibility of it has been denied for contemporary experience, and the existence of it has been denied in historical retrospect. The two *dementis* would seem to be connected — if we permit ourselves the argument *post hoc, ergo propter hoc* which sometimes suffices for historical relations — since this paired negation follows upon the paired affirmation by nineteenth-century historians who had more confidence than we in the general possibility of beneficent political guidance from above and who were more insistent than we upon the authentic existence of enlightened despotism in the eighteenth century. But if, as the parallelogram would seem to indicate, the current skeptical historical thesis is as politically conditioned as the older credulous historical thesis, and if ideally this correspondence should give us pause, the fact is that we proceed on our belief both in the superior validity of our own political assumptions and in the larger autonomy of our historical judgments. The demythologizing impact of the recent satrapical totalitarianism leads us to believe that our contemporaries are more perceptive about politics in general than were our nineteenth-century predecessors; and we have subliminally absorbed enough of the scientist's faith in the cumulative progress of knowledge along with our investment in a science of history to believe that our more comprehensive information about what in the eighteenth century was classified as enlightened despotism by the nineteenth is not only bigger but also better than the select data in the neatly labeled depositories of our forebears.

Certainly we can no longer subscribe to the literal historical sense of enlightened despotism—that is, to a distinctive phase and mode of absolutism, dominant in Europe during the second half of the eighteenth century, consonant with the orderly commercializing society emergent in that age, which qualified internally the externally unconditioned power of autocracy with an essential disposition to exercise government on the basis of the best contemporary knowledge, in accordance with rational planning, and for the attainment of socially benevolent goals. Such was the familiar historiographical meaning which was retrospectively visited upon the eighteenth century by monarchically and systematically minded German historians of the nineteenth. These original spokesmen for what we may well call the traditional view of enlightened despotism—a view that prevailed without essential question through the first third of the twentieth century—varied the particular qualities which they attributed to the rubric but concerted on its general form. Wilhelm Roscher, political economist of the historical school, set the tone by coining the historiographical usage of "enlightened despot" in 1847 and by developing it during the second half of the century into a full-blown theory of "enlightened absolute monarchy," conceived as the third and final stage of a progressive absolutism which was produced by natural laws of social evolution. Heinrich von Treitschke, patriotic historian of increasingly authoritarian stamp, explicitly exalted "enlightened despotism" into "a new idea of the State," a Germanically sponsored type and phase of responsible autocracy modeled by Frederick the Great. Reinhold Koser, political historian especially committed to Prussia of the old regime, epitomized Roscher's "enlightened absolute monarchy" as "enlightened despotism" without commenting on the linguistic alteration, and he inverted its meaning from a monarchical progression to a monarchical "regression" without disturbing its status as a fundamental stage in the history of politics.[1] Common to these formulators of the tradition and to the consensus they prefigured were the accepted equivalence of enlightened despotism and enlightened absolutism and the interchangeable use of either to denote the identifiable and characteristic system of eighteenth-century continental government.

But since the appearance of a politically critical, self-conscious, revisionist historiography during the 1930s, the traditional interpretation has been subject to a many-sided attack. Historians have brought several centrifuges, both practical and theoretical, to bear against the historical unity which this interpretation has represented. They have stressed the actual varieties of eighteenth-century political practice, even in the hands of monarchs presumably uniform in their enlightenment. They have applied to the eighteenth century our own hardly won experience of the conservative practical reality that so often persists behind the enlightened rhetoric of reform. They have been led by this experience to be especially aware of the factual limits which historic corporations, bureaucratic agencies, the cake of custom, and sheer physical restrictions upon communication and control still imposed upon nominal autocrats in the eighteenth century. Those historians who take theory seriously have drawn increasing attention to the gap between the articulate political ideas of the liberal philosophes and the model of enlightened despotism. And with their increasing sophistication about political philosophy, historians have ever more insistently drawn a logical distinction between enlightened despotism and enlightened absolutism.

Of these critical adductions, the latter two—evidence of overt hostility to the theory of enlightened despotism in the

eighteenth century, and the discrimination between absolutism
and despotism by historians of the twentieth — merit our special
attention, because they have implications that carry beyond the
ostensible target of their criticism and adumbrate a new stage
in the discussion. Certainly the signal eighteenth-century
expressions of aversion to "enlightened despots" or other
cognates of enlightened despotism have become memorable;
and there is no reason to think that these expressions are not as
representative of the intellectual class who made theory as they
are usually deemed to be, especially since this articulate
anti-absolutism reflected a radicalization of attitude that
coincided with the expansion of political theorizing as such in
the generation before the French Revolution. But we should
note, for reconsideration later (p. 44 below), that much of the
explicit rejection of enlightened despotism came from men who
had also, at one time or another, endorsed the notion. The
repeated supersession militates strongly against the traditional
view of a dominant enlightened despotism, but it leaves open
the historical meaning of the transitory enlightened despotism
they did endorse.

The pattern includes some of the best-known names in the
Enlightenment.[2] Before 1770 Diderot had celebrated in correspondence and in personal contacts the prevalence and
power of the "philosopher-prince" in the Europe of his day. But
by 1774 he was arguing to Catherine the Great, in an express
reference to enlightened despotism which was rare for the
eighteenth century but would become notorious for posterity,
that "two or three consecutive reigns of a just and enlightened
despotism" would be "one of the great misfortunes that could
occur to any free nation," since any despot, "be he the best of
men, . . . is a good shepherd who reduces his subjects to the
level of animals," habituating them to "blind obedience" and
securing them "a happiness of ten years for which they would
pay with twenty centuries of misery." Raynal, in whose work
Diderot collaborated closely, exhibited the same kind of development to the general reading public. In the original edition of
his *Histoire philosophique et politique des établissements et du*

commerce des Européens dans les deux Indes, published in 1770, Raynal's only reference to enlightened despotism was in approving terms that were addressed to the specific condition of "uncivilized peoples" but seemed flexible enough for expanded application to any unenlightened society. "Given their lack of experience, which alone forms reason, and their incapacity to rule themselves . . . , government ought to be enlightened for them and to direct them with its authority to the age of enlightenment. Thus uncivilized peoples find themselves naturally under the reins and the rod of despotism until the progress of society has taught them to conduct themselves in accordance with their own interests." But thenceforward each of Raynal's editions would be more radical than the preceding. By 1773 he had added a volume on the contemporary state of Europe and on the general principles derivative therefrom. These principles were more categorically libertarian than the comparatively qualified and moderate discussions of colonial materials that preceded them. Now he discussed enlightened despotism as such and in general; and his approach was entirely negative. "You will hear it said that the happiest government would be that of a just and enlightened despot," he wrote in acknowledgment of a current opinion, presumably Physiocratic. But he introduced the opinion only to use it as a foil, and he rejected it along lines almost identical with Diderot's. By 1780 Raynal's condemnation was even more dramatic: "A first just, resolute, and enlightened despot is a great evil; a second just, resolute, and enlightened despot would be a greater evil; a third who would succeed them with these same qualities would be the most terrible scourge with which a nation could be struck." Not only was the language of the judgment stronger but Raynal added a further revealing ground of it. It was not simply the insidious increment of violation that comes from the beneficence of the violator but also — more damningly — "the impossibility for the despot himself, even . . . the most completely enlightened and the most zealous for the welfare of his people," to do anything at all effective for "the liberation, or what is the same thing under another name, the civilization of an Empire." Certainly there was a direct contradiction between the specific Raynal who believed in the civilizing capacity of despotism and the general Raynal who did not (for the specific approval of enlightened despotism for primitives continued to be carried in the same editions that denounced enlightened despotism for anybody), but there was a dialectical element in the final version of Raynal's general rejection that gives it a historical interest beyond mere contradiction. Raynal added the quality "resolute" to the just and enlightened despot at the same time as he was adding impotence to the quality of the despot's action. Thereby Raynal gave expression to the problematical belief in the essential debility of political force that would help to drive others to a redefinition of enlightened despotism and that should help to guide us to a reconsideration of enlightened despotism.

The instability of theoretical enlightened despotism was evident not only in those like Diderot and Raynal who made passing references to it but also in those like Mercier de la Rivière, doctrinaire theorist of the Physiocratic version of enlightened despotism that became notorious during the eighteenth century itself as "legal despotism." For Mercier himself dropped the idea after the formula met with widespread protest, most trenchantly phrased in Rousseau's stricture against the "two contradictory words which, put together, mean nothing to me." Again, despite his own Physiocratic sympathies and authoritarian administrative activities, Turgot, chief agent of and sometime spokesman for a reforming absolutism in France, warned against the alienating and obfuscating effect of "that devil, 'despotism,'" in the Physiocratic formula. Indeed, the whole line of respectable intellectuals from Voltaire to Kant whose admiration of one autocrat or another, epitomized in Frederick the Great's own claim to a just and virtuous despotic power and in Kant's identification of "the century of Frederick" with "the age of enlightenment," helped to give enlightened despotism whatever good resonance it has had, ultimately corrected themselves with their overt substitution (in Kant's version) of "the representative system" for the "enlightened prince" as the preferred alternative to unenlightened "despotism."

It should be clear from even such a casual collection of critical reasons that the effect of historical revision has gone beyond the category of enlightened despotism to undermine as well the concept of "enlightened absolutism," which until recently seemed an acceptable reduced alternative to sophisticated students of the subject.[3] Now this elevation of doubt to the second power extends the issue from corrections of political logic and terminology to questions of historical substance. If we recall the age-old distinction in political theory between despotism as arbitrary government with no limits and absolutism as legitimate government with no humanly enforceable limits, then it should be clear that the logical difficulty of affixing an enlightened qualification to an unqualifiable despotism does not hold for an absolutism which had for long had definitive qualities built into its very concept: "enlightened" qualities needed only to be substituted for traditional ones. There remains, to be sure, the urgent question of whether the enlightened qualities—that is, qualities associated with the political culture of the eighteenth-century Enlightenment— were compatible with absolutism, but this kind of compatibility was, and is now commonly deemed to be, a matter of fact rather than of reason. In the fruitful century of political philosophizing that began with Hobbes and ran through Montesquieu, after all, there had been ample demonstration of the theoretical compatibility between absolutism and the concern for individual rights that was so prominent a part of the Enlightened creed. Unlike the stricture upon enlightened despotism, where it is argued that there were eighteenth-century men who asserted it but could not have meant what they asserted, the modern critic of enlightened absolutism admits that eighteenth-century men *could have* associated absolutism with their enlightened values but he insists that they *did not* in fact characteristically do so, either because the intellectuals did not make the association in theory, or because the politicians did not live it in practice, or both.

This extension of criticism from the term "enlightened

despotism" to the concept of enlightened absolutism is more than the revision of a revision. Where "enlightened despotism" is an ostensive phrase, calling for the traditional discriminating criticism of particular texts, enlightened absolutism is an imputed category, postulated to unify overtly heterogeneous eighteenth-century political facts. With the spread of doubt from the phrase to the category, the consensus on a specific illusion has yielded to the historiographical plurality attendant upon the dissolution of a historical general type. In this enlarged critical context "enlightened despotism" is no longer a problem unto itself but becomes rather an especially vulnerable specimen of the larger problem of enlightened absolutism, illustrating literally the inviability of the concept and the heterogeneity of the presumed type.

But there is one level of approximate concordance among the disputant historians on the conjoint problem of enlightened despotism and enlightened absolutism: there is general agreement, by and large, on the historical ingredients of the problem. These may be summarized as follows:

As a literal idea — when it is deemed to have been nothing but a literal idea — "enlightened despotism" was espoused during the 1760s and 1770s only by the French Physiocrats, who built it into a theory they did not really mean, and in brief isolated invocations by eccentrics like Raynal or Holbach, who were too inconsistent ever to mean anything in politics; otherwise, "enlightened despotism" was rejected by those few eighteenth-century intellectuals who paid any attention to it at all. As a definitely implied doctrine, enlightened absolutism was espoused only by the German and Austrian Cameralists of the later eighteenth century — notably J. G. von Justi and Josef von Sonnenfels — whose impact in this respect was minimal. As an indefinitely implied belief, enlightened absolutism was the temporary and tactical persuasion of those who, like Voltaire and Diderot, wrote sentimental testimonials to, or requested particular initiatives of, their favored monarchs at the moments they were favored. As a matter of political principle, enlightened absolutism was the ad hoc rhetoric adopted by literate rulers of central and eastern Europe who used it selectively as an instrument of policy contingent upon more fundamental political concerns. As a stage in the development of western politics, enlightened absolutism is thinkable only in reference to a group of later eighteenth-century, central and eastern European reforming monarchs whose dissimilarities of policy were at least as prominent as their similarities and whose status as representatives of a distinctive historical type or stage remains dubious.

The consensus on the historical components of enlightened absolutism breaks down with the assessments of what these components add up to. For the criticism of enlightened absolutism as an essential general truth of late eighteenth-century life is not the simple matter of aye or nay that the literal denial of enlightened despotism has been. Because enlightened absolutism is a presumably viable composite, the criticism of it has taken the form not of negating its historical validity but of dissolving its historical integrity. Even historians who generally frown upon the historiographical separation of ideas from actions have affirmed the historical independence of the theory from the practice of enlightened absolutism in the eighteenth century, and enlightened absolutism as such — that is, as a historical type — becomes a casualty of the tenuous relationships between its theory and its practice. Previous discussion has produced five distinct, if sometimes overlapping, relationships between theory and practice in reference to enlightened absolutism — aside from the superseded simple and positive correlation between the theory and practice of an authentic enlightened absolutism — and each entails a variantly material, if invariantly pejorative, definition of what enlightened absolutism historically was.

One relationship posits an enlightened absolutist theory and a merely absolutist practice.[4] The theory of enlightened absolutism here is a tautology, since enlightened absolutism cannot in this case be anything but a theory; and enlightened absolutism as a historical type becomes a rhetorical flourish.

A second relationship posits a liberal humanitarian theory

and an enlightened absolutist practice.[5] The theory of enlightened absolutism here is a nullity, since enlightened absolutism existed only on the level of practice, *faute de mieux*, and would have been something quite other as a theory; and enlightened absolutism as a historical type becomes only an incoherent compromise between divergent ideas and conditions.

A third relationship posits a liberal humanitarian theory and a merely absolutist practice.[6] Enlightened absolutism here becomes a convenient fiction, imputing a conceptual stability and identity to the plurality of transitory and particular policy recommendations that inhabited the eighteenth-century reformers' shadow world between theory and practice.

A fourth relationship posits a theory that was neither absolutist nor liberal because it was essentially nonpolitical and a practice that was neither enlightened nor absolutist because it was essentially pragmatic.[7] Here enlightened absolutism gets the double whammy, for it becomes the nontheory of a nonentity.

A fifth relationship, finally, posits a tenuous connection between enlightenment and absolutism within both the theory and the practice of enlightened absolutism. Here the tension between enlightened individualism and authoritarian absolutism in theory becomes a reflection of the overlap of social mobility and social stasis in practice, and enlightened absolutism stands for the unstable transition between traditional and modern society.[8]

But with the exploration of this fifth relationship, which is the focus of the most recent research, the comparative advantage of enlightened absolutism over enlightened despotism, resting as this advantage does on the norm of consistency, is lost, and we find now a prevalent apposition of the term "enlightened despotism" with the concept of enlightened absolutism in the usage of sophisticated modern historians who are fully aware of the distinction between the pejorative term which has not been a historiographical problem and the credible concept which has become one.[9] This persistence in an atavistic phraseology may well be attributable in part to the taxonomic inertia which is so often diagnosed to be an occupational disease of historians, whether it is viewed critically as a substitute for thinking or sympathetically as a still generally recognizable label for a diffusive period otherwise not denotable at all. But the addiction to enlightened despotism has other, more essential, reasons as well—reasons relating negatively to the inadequacies of enlightened absolutism as an alternative and positively to some emergent implications of "enlightened despotism" which go toward its rehabilitation.

The fact is that enlightened absolutism does not work at all as a paradigm whose authoritative meaning should be inferred from the contemporary political language of the eighteenth century, and it has not been very satisfactory as a category which applies our subsequently superior wisdom about politics and human nature retrospectively to the understanding of what eighteenth-century men must have really meant.[10] Enlightened absolutism is invalid as a paradigm because eighteenth-century man was relatively indifferent to the idea of political absolutism per se (as to all fundamental concepts of political structure vis-à-vis political function) and was ambiguous about its meaning when he did mention it in the derivative form of an adjectival cognate. Unlike "despotism," which was politically current throughout the eighteenth century, the term absolut*ism* acquired its political signification only toward 1800, preparatory to its prominent career during the nineteenth century. Effectively, if not reflectively, as important as the absence of a term for the political concept was the absence of a term for the political agent: the substantive "absolutist" seems awkward and contrived in any case, but unlike "despot," which has a linguistic history going back to Aristotle and served as root for eighteenth-century "despotism," "absolutist" has been a derivative of "absolutism" and had no more currency in the eighteenth century than did its parent term.

Eighteenth-century writers did make political application of the adjective "absolute" as an attribute of power, but their subordinate and variable use of it in this capacity confirms the salience of their failure to develop the notion of absolute power into the dominant factor of a distinctive political system, such as is usually connoted by the hypostatization of a tendency into an ism. The inconspicuous place which "absolute" held in the eighteenth-century grammar of politics is attested not only negatively, by its absence from the capital genera of such standard sources as the *Spirit of the Laws*, the *Encyclopédie*, and the *Social Contract* — and the kind and degree of attention accorded to ideas are as relevant to their meaning as their content is — but also by its dependent associations and divergent meanings in the remote passages where it was to be found. Political power was characterized as "absolute" in three different contexts with three vitally different meanings, which, either because they were too broad or too narrow, shared the single common feature of denying a distinctive definition to the absolute quality.

For writers otherwise as unlike as Blackstone and Rousseau, absolute power was equivalent to political authority as such and applied to every valid form of government. In Rousseau's casual figure: "Just as nature gives each man an absolute power [*pouvoir absolu*] over all his limbs, just so the social pact gives the body politic an absolute power over all its members; and it is this same power, which, directed by the general will, bears . . . the title of sovereignty."[11] This indiscriminate absolute power has limits, but they are merely the indefinite constituent limits of the body politic as such.

A second group — including such uncomfortable set-fellows as Diderot, Holbach, and Bentham — carried on the traditional usage of "absolute power" or "absolute sovereignty" as the constitutional designation for "unlimited" vis-à-vis "limited" government, but in such a way as to minimize both the importance and the force of the distinction. Not only were these categories afforded a subsidiary position in the argumentation, but the difference between them was usually deemed to be a matter merely of the absence or presence of "express laws" or "express conventions" which assigned additional special limits to sovereignty over and above "the fundamental laws" of the state and the factual or "natural limits" of reason and equity which were binding upon absolute and limited sovereignty alike. Whether or not the "express laws" which distinguished limited from absolute power were identified by necessity and in principle with the constitutional division rather than an institutional circumscription of sovereign powers — and this identification varied from writer to writer, and even from occasion to occasion in the same writer — the distinction was not deemed crucial. When Diderot wrote about power and sovereignty, he minimized the difference between their absolute and limited versions by emphasizing both the danger and the futility of legally enforceable limits, and he stressed the self-limitation of absolute monarchs; when he elaborated upon representative government, he dropped his original classification of absolute monarchies, where the king was representative of the nation, and limited monarchies, where the king shares this capacity with elected representatives of the nation, essentially by merging both kinds of monarchy into a single class vis-à-vis "despotic states," where there is no representative of the nation. Even in his *Politique naturelle*, where Holbach acknowledged the "express laws" which prescribed the constitutional division of the sovereign power, he insisted that the sundry shares of this power added up to "absolute authority" nonetheless, and he focused on the "natural limits" rather than on the adventitious constitution of such authority. But it was Bentham who was perhaps the most ingenuous about the function of the "express convention" which limited the otherwise "indefinite" power of the "supreme governor," for he characterized its function to be simply the provision of a "common signal," marking the limits of the subjects' "disposition to obedience" and serving merely to guide them in their calculations of the utility of submitting or resisting.[12]

The third connotation of absolute power, even more divergent from the other two than those two were from each other, adjoined it to arbitrary power as a metonym for despotism. The striking feature of this usage, reinforcing the inconstancy of the political attitude toward the absolute apparent in the very fact of its triple meaning, was its employment in this third, pejorative, sense within the works which included its more neutral applications. The *Encyclopédie*, which featured Diderot's nominal distinction between despotism and absolute monarchy, also contained the definition of the one in terms of the other. In his article, "Despotism," Diderot's friend and collaborator Louis de Jaucourt characterized it as the "tyrannical, arbitrary, and absolute government of one man" which comports with his "taking an absolute power over the possessions of all men."[13] Despite his deliberate admission of absolute monarchy to the legitimate ranks of governments which are conditioned by natural and fundamental laws, Holbach also repeatedly, albeit casually, used "absolute monarch," "absolute sovereign," and "absolute power" as synonyms for "arbitrary power," "despot," and "despotism."[14] Even Rousseau, as categorical as he was in the attribution of absolute power to every body politic and in his assurance that "as absolute . . . as the sovereign power is it does not and cannot pass the limits of its constituent general conventions," could not avoid slipping into the derogatory—and inconsistent—signification of "absolute" when he asserted that no valid constituent convention would "stipulate absolute authority on one side and unlimited obedience on the other."[15]

The equivocal political meaning of "absolute" in eighteenth-century usage may well have been connected with the extrinsicality of absolutism as an eighteenth-century political idea, since neither as a term nor as an idea was it vouchsafed a determinative attention. But in any case the sources give no support to absolutism as the defining structure of an eighteenth-century political model. Nor are we better off with an absolutist model if we consider it purely as a retrospective category. For it has retained at least a double meaning, connoting both the distinction from arbitrary power that was developed before the eighteenth century for the political theory of unlimited monarchy in response to the traditional extraconstitutional limits upon autocratic power, and the sense of a totally unconditioned and arbitrary—that is, despotic—power that our growing disbelief in the efficacy of any unenforceable checks upon political power has extended to all constitutionally unlimited political systems ever since the eighteenth century. Thus the concept of absolutism with which recent historiography has measured eighteenth-century political thought and behavior has been as ambivalent as the shifty linguistic testimony about absolute power. Historians may now be more self-conscious about absolutism and more sophisticated about models than were their eighteenth-century sources, but we still vacillate between the imputation of a self-limiting absolutism whose juncture with enlightened values was a possibility of the age and the imputation of an arbitrary absolutism, complementary to the "despotic" terminology of the age and functioning as the implicit pattern of assumptions about the nature of unlimited government which gives this terminology its political meaning.[16]

The persistent ambiguity of absolutism sets obvious limits upon its historiographical usefulness as a category, but over and above this inconvenience its value has been defined by its largely negative incidence. In both of its versions, the concept of absolutism has been applied to demonstrate the restricted validity or the invalidity of enlightened absolutism as a paradigm of eighteenth-century deed and thought, whether because the variety of eighteenth-century life actually exceeded the implicit unity of the composite concept or because the testimony of eighteenth-century men literally rejected or circuited the explicit despotic cognates of the implicit absolutist unity. Recent substitutions of "enlightened government," "enlightened bureaucracy," and "enlightened monarchy" for enlightened absolutism as alternatives to enlightened despotism accurately reflect the conviction of historians that the concepts appropriate to the consistent association of enlightenment and politics in the eighteenth century must be more formal, more manifold, or more partial than the substantive political system connoted by enlightened absolutism.[17]

For the historians who persist in referring to "enlightened despotism" as a characteristic syndrome of the later eighteenth century despite all the arguments that can be invoked against it from political logic, linguistic analysis, and historical fact, a more positive ground can be averred than the inadequacy of enlightened absolutism or the political indifference of its blander replacements. "Enlightened despotism" is retained precisely because of its much-mooted self-contradictoriness — because it, and only it, faithfully reflects the relations of unity and heterogeneity in eighteenth-century life by acknowledging the indefeasible reality of both. Enlightened absolutism, and its milder surrogates *a fortiori*, predicates a systematic political norm which is imputed by historians to the eighteenth century but from which the evidence (including the dubious eighteenth-century attitudes toward "enlightened despotism") marks so many departures in eighteenth-century reality. Under the new historiographical dispensation enlightened despotism predicates the common acknowledgment by historians and eighteenth-century historical agents alike of both the original contrariety of human circumstances and an equally essential correlativity in human institutions, a duality articulated in composite devices which were set up in the eighteenth century to relate the discordant elements of such a divided existence sufficiently to make it a thinkable and livable reality.[18]

But if this common ground justifies the figurative attribution of enlightened despotism to eighteenth-century agents by twentieth-century historians it also obscures a crucial difference in the respective orientations of the two groups, and this difference must be borne in mind to avoid anachronism: whereas men in the twentieth century think of political incoherence as *the* essential reality which can be transcended only through an ideal projected beyond the reality, men in the eighteenth century thought of it as *a* reality subsisting alongside of another, more orderly reality with which it had to be connected.

The question which naturally arises at this point is: how does the reinstated category of enlightened despotism differ from the traditional idea of it which has been so impressively refuted by the literal evidence of the confusing variety in the eighteenth-century usages of "despot" and "despotism" and of the preponderant contemporary rejection of a specifically "enlightened despotism" on the comparatively few occasions of its explicit usage? The answer can best be given in two parts, one methodological and one substantial, to indicate the point of view from which the material receives its postcritical interpretation.

In point of method, enlightened despotism is one of those ideas with a dual historiographical status which is distorted by either of the standard singular hermeneutics and with which we are only just learning to cope. The standard hermeneutics include, on the one hand, the prescription for ascertaining the literal contemporary meaning of the explicit language used by historical agents and, on the other, the prescription for imputing subsequently discovered or clarified concepts and categories to historical agents for the unintended meaning of what they have thought and done. Both of these hermeneutics have been applied to eighteenth-century enlightened despotism, with the salutary critical results of which we are all aware. But there is a hybrid kind of historical material—to which enlightened despotism belongs—which is susceptible to a third kind of approach, more ambiguous and more indirect than either of the other two. This is the kind of material which is both sign and symbol: it both has a literal reference for the historical agents who produced it and is symptomatic of a more diffused and inchoate attitude which may have a resonance and a bearing quite other than the immediate contexts of the explicit term. The term "enlightened despotism" is thus allusive to rather than representative of the unspoken attitude it crystallizes. Frequently enough, as the familiar examples of "party" in the eighteenth century and "ideology" in the early nineteenth attest, an express pejorative covers a more fundamental descriptive meaning.

Since this methodological situation is liable to be obscured by the fashionable terminology that has recently been devised to deal with deceptively similar situations, let us restate the case in terms of such classificatory nomenclature. The label "paradigm" has been appropriated especially to mark the standard hermeneutics of an intellectual model which is constructed from the contemporary language. The label "category" best denotes the standard hermeneutics of a general concept which spans periods through imputation and is retrospectively applied. Neither is precisely appropriate to the temporal mix which conditions ideas like enlightened despotism. What is appropriate to such intermediate judgments that have a basis in contemporary usage but also transcend it is most aptly fixed by the label "schema" in the Kantian sense of a synthesis mediatory between the empirical and the categorical and enabling the organization of the literal manifold under unifying concepts.[19]

In the case of "enlightened despotism," historians' persistent reference to it as a general category of eighteenth-century politics despite their awareness of its dubious literal standing in the century may well express their feeling that the deliberate illogicality of the term captures an eighteenth-century state of mind that far transcends, both linguistically and conceptually, the specific contexts of the term itself. Like the iceberg effect, the term becomes a revealing outcropping of a far-ranging set of assumptions that hypostatized discordance rather than unity as the fundamental constellation of eighteenth-century politics and made the management of discord rather than the application of unity the function of political principle. "Enlightened despotism" is thus now not merely a political theory of admittedly limited resonance but also a schema which covers more than the theory, is denoted by a variety of terms exceeding the language of the theory, and is relatively indifferent to the instability and low repute of that theory. As schema, it extends to every theoretical and practical situation where there was a recognized and inherent dissonance between the tendencies of the political instruments at hand and the nature of the social goals to be achieved by them and yet where some linkage was nonetheless strung up between instruments and goals. The literal theory, in this syndrome, is but an indicator of the larger concept, accorded the titular honor in this essay not for its prevalence but for its hyperbolic pairing of obviously uncongenial factors. As a historiographical category, "enlightened despotism" covers not only the literal eighteenth-century assertions of the theory which illustrate some linking devices but also the literal eighteenth-century rejections of the theory which underline the basic heterogeneity of the elements involved in the linkage. And the concept covers too, of course, analogous literal pairings, in whatever terminology they appeared during the eighteenth century, so long as they were accompanied by the awareness of an essential illogicality in their relations.

Under this methodological dispensation, the conduit from the literal "enlightened despotism" of admittedly narrow literal range to the broader schematic attitude it connoted runs through the sundry notions of "despot" and "despotism," which, unlike absolutism, constituted literally a capital division and primary concern in the eighteenth-century writings about politics. Those notions were not only mentioned but theoretically developed in these writings, and they were multiform enough to serve as the point of juncture between what was literal and what was intellectual—that is, between words and ideas.[20]

It is, indeed, with the variegated eighteenth-century usage of "despot" and "despotism" that the substantial insights that are afforded by the schematic approach to "enlightened despotism" begin to become apparent. For although the terms' wide range of meanings in eighteenth-century literature has been abundantly documented,[21] the upshot of the variety for the substantive "despotism" is not the ambiguity of the adjectival "absolute" but a convergence of meanings that renders the superficially contradictory qualification of it as "enlightened" not only explicable in itself but representative of a comprehensible larger attitude.

The plurality of meanings which had been associated with the terms "despot" and "despotic" since the ancient Greeks— the terms were used to characterize both the social power of the master, as the head of the extended household, over his slaves

(later, of the lord over his serfs) and the analogously unre-
strained political power of a ruler over his disfranchised or
unfranchised subjects — undoubtedly did persist through the
eighteenth century, and, as has been emphatically maintained,
some of this traditional variety undoubtedly did rub off on the
neological "despotism." When "despot" and "despotic," which
had been used to indicate a quality in various kinds of power,
were hypostatized in the term "despotism," the noun came to
indicate, in various forms, a dominant principle in a definite
system of government, with a presumed oriental model pro-
viding the definition and a universal applicability grounding
the system.[22] Ostensibly the views of this system could differ as
radically as Bayle's and Voltaire's dispassionate position on despotism as a standard governing genre with its own definitive
qualities did from Montesquieu's widely shared alternate indict-
ments of despotism as a "government . . . in which a single person directs everything by his own will and caprice" and as the
"degenerate" form of all forms of government, whether by the
one, the few, or the many.[23] Ostensibly, again, a Diderot, a
Jaucourt, and a Holbach could retain Montesquieu's trans-
mission of the seventeenth century's caricature of a despotic
oriental politics and be either gently corrected by the understanding religious approach of a Nicolas-Antoine Boulanger
(in his *Recherches sur l'origine du despotisme oriental*) or
violently opposed by the insistence of a Voltaire or an Anquetil-
Duperron upon the categorical incongruity of the oriental
reality with the model of capricious despotism.[24]

But what was novel and distinctive in the eighteenth-century
approach to the idea of the despot through the political
principle of despotism was the paradoxical sense which came to
be made of its divergent meanings. It is hardly an accident that
the antisystematic critics who were most keenly attuned to the
anomalies of the age and the less skeptical publicists in their
most paradoxical moods were precisely the ones most favor-
ably — and maliciously — disposed to see in the idea of despotism a way of rationalizing the anomalies of the age precisely
because it did reflect them in comprehensible form. Thus

Simon-Nicolas-Henri Linguet, the caustic maverick of the late Enlightenment who delighted in debunking the false logic of his liberal colleagues, defined sovereigns in the authentic, traditional despotic terms of "proprietors" of their states who "can do everything in their states that a paterfamilias can do in his household." He announced his preference for such a "government, stigmatized through our thoughtlessness by the odious name of despotism," on very modern grounds — its interference "on behalf of the people, that is, the most numerous and weakest part of the nation."[25] Similarly, August Ludwig von Schlözer, the journalistic *enfant terrible* of the Germanies who also modernized Cameralism by developing the science of administrative statistics, meant to shock but took into full account the centrifugal contemporary tendencies represented by the newer instruments of public power and the recent demands for civil liberties when he defined "sovereignty" (*HerrscherRecht*) as "this unlimited force which acts in the final instance without other control" and declared boldly that "if this be called despotism, then every government, every state . . . is despotic." He declared the only remedy against the abuse of this inevitably despotic power to be a plurality of organs to exercise it.[26]

However isolated these eccentrics may have been and however rhetorical their adoption of despotism, the feature of it which they revealed — its theoretical capacity to house incompatibilities — was confirmed by the essential qualities attributed to despotism by the myriad publicists who announced their abhorrence of it. What was common to these rejections of despotism for its excess of power was the perverse insistence upon its real limits — upon the actual self-limitation built into the very nature of the system. For those who, like Bayle and Voltaire, revised the illusory model of an infinitely capricious despotism by calling attention to the ubiquity of institutional or customary molds, the case is clear enough. What needs stress is the undue attention paid to the inherent weakness and restrictions of the despotic system by the very same men who defined it in general by its provision of an indefinitely excessive power.

When they were in their empirical, historical gear, both Montesquieu and Condillac, those pacesetters of Enlightenment, insisted upon the de facto limits of despotism, from the commonsense view of the obvious physical and social impossibility that "any human authority be despotic in every respect." As Montesquieu declared in his Roman history: "the greatest power is always limited by some angle [*coin*]."[27]

Their followers were more categorical in their abstract definition of despotism as unconditionally arbitrary government, but they also went further in demonstrating the actual impotence of the despot in a political system of despotism because of his inevitable dependence upon his guard and his "vizier" (the collective label, with due oriental connotation, for devolutionary royal ministers), and because of the equally inevitable immobility, recalcitrance, or resistance of his subjects.[28] "Despotism generates revolutions," Turgot opined, and he applied this natural law of politics both to military coups and to the "total revolution" of the alienated people.[29]

In part, to be sure, this emphasis was overtly tactical: it intentionally warned princes to avoid despotism in their own interest. In part too the emphasis was traditionally rhetorical: it restated the lesson about the wages of political sin in the old genre of the royal educational manual, setting up the infirmity of the despot as the horrible negation of the strength accruing to the paternalistic and virtuous prince of familiar mien.[30]

But the notice of a paradoxical despotic debility also had reference to a far deeper and more significant mentality. In general, it is a mistake to treat the circumstantial and rhetorical expedients so frequently proposed during the eighteenth century as so many departures from or replacements of political principle. Certainly the bulk of the politically interested public subscribed to Pope's well-known adage that "whate'er is best administered is best," but if this utilitarian subscription indicated an indifference to the more deductive forms of political theorizing it did not indicate an indifference to political theorizing as such.[31] Political principle was not abandoned; it was relocated. Given the eighteenth-century intellectuals' penchant for ad hoc generalization, the very fact that practical and rhetorical considerations were deemed important enough to make old-style abstract theorizing irrelevant drew these considerations themselves into the theoretical vacuum thus created, establishing them as the respectable ingredients of political principle-making in a new mode. Thus the popularity of despotism as a political category was precisely its function of elevating the relative measurement of government by result into a steady principle. Each of the varied approaches to despotism was triggered by circumstance — advocacy of it by relations with a particular ruler or by the urgency of a particular reform, the rejection of it by the souring of relations or the address of monarchical power to violation of the wrong rights, the condescension toward it by hortatory design — and each also manifested principle. Thus for Jaucourt the devolution of power to the vizier was not simply an observation of fact but "the consequence of the fundamental principle of despotic states."[32] Dupont de Nemours recognized that the contemporary combination, under the single term "despot," of the idea of someone who "disposes of things as he wishes [*a son gré*]" with the idea of "arbitrary sovereigns," who "can dispose of nothing, or at least of very little," was not a mere inconsistency but an "implied contradiction."[33]

What Dupont did not recognize was that this contradiction in principle was built into the very notion of eighteenth-century "despotism" and accounted for its true meaning. The various senses of despotism were associated by the paradoxical awareness that the effective quantity of political power varied directly with the imposition of controls to channel and direct it. Despotism had to be self-limiting not because, like absolute sovereignty, it was conditionally constituted but because it was conditionally operative. In a very real sense, then, despotism must be enlightened or not be at all. Such was implied, certainly, by the resultant of the various meanings of despotism — the notion of it as an especially intensive and comprehensive kind of autocracy, unbounded by any rights vested in its subjects but inevitably and paradoxically self-defeating by reliance upon the sovereign will-to-power alone and operable only by deliberate alliance with the available sources of social and natural force in the world.

The most linear assertions of the alliance between the effective force of monarchical government and the rational mobilization of social resources came, as might be expected, from German Cameralists and their successors. Justi insisted that "the true, transcendent power of a state" (*die wahren Macht und Übermacht eines Staats*) derived from the existence of "a well-considered plan and firmly established principles," operated solely by the "ruler" (*Regent*) who thus "has in his hands the whole system of government with all its particular branches and every class of business" since these are all "connected" into the general system.[34] Justi's oft-cited analogy of the state with "a machine in which all the wheels and gears are precisely adjusted to one another" and of the ruler with "the foreman, the mainspring, or the soul ... which sets everything in motion"[35] should be read in the context for which he designed it — the necessary concatenation of rational planning and authoritarian direction for the maximization of political power.

Where the Cameralists made governmental power proportional to the deliberate mobilization of social resources, the Physiocrats made it dependent upon the knowledgeable employment of the forces of nature. The most impressive testimony of this dependence as the only alternative to political impotence came from Turgot. He, perhaps because he was more a fellow traveler than a card-carrying Physiocrat, did not quite so readily assume an integral connection between the law of nature and the law of the sovereign, and was more wary of literal "despotism" as essentially non-Western (the Roman Empire was despotic in principle but not in practice). By dint of his reservations Turgot was more revealing of the assumptions behind the more doctrinaire Physiocrats, who were more literally assertive. In Turgot the paradox of eighteenth-century politics was mirrored precisely. He insisted both that in political principle the "spirit of system" was false and that in political fact government was a "chaos," dominated by "too many objects," "too many positive institutions of different vintages," "too many corporations with different interests and privileges," "too many tribunals," "too many special administrative departments," for decisions not to be usually—and disastrously—determined by "special circumstances" rather than "fundamental principle" or "general plan." Hence he also insisted both that government must not be intrusive and that men in general were "too limited in their views, too trivial in their interests, nearly always too opposed to one another in seeking out their particular welfare," not to require "a superior power to conciliate so many different interests and direct them toward the same end."[36] Turgot ultimately found a specific resolution in his relationship of constitutionalism to the doctrine of political sovereignty, as we shall see below,[37] but behind this resolution lay a mode of thought which found in nature the potent order unavailable in politics as such. When Turgot represented his "image of sovereignty" as "that universal agent of nature, the water . . . for which there must be mountains whose slope . . ., by directing the course of the waters, distributes their benefits," the choice of physical figure was something more than mere metaphor: it betrayed his tendency to consider effective force in government as a literal alliance with nature. For in his plan for a science of political geography Turgot concluded that "in the long run political geography prevails over public law." "Because real order is only in the whole [*ensemble*] of things and because the whole is too vast for our senses" when we view the fluvial action of the earth, in our own irrigations we do not so much "supplement nature" as "replace it," and "the only possible way" to do this is "to imitate it."[38]

But for the explicit application of the problematic relations between knowledge and political power to the concept of "despotism" we had best turn to Helvétius, Mirabeau, and Holbach, whose ambivalent attitude toward this concept produced a tortuous kind of thinking more precisely reflective of its tenuous redefinition into a necessarily enlightened despotism. The smooth assertion of a doubled enlightenment for true monarchs, at once passive and active—they should themselves be "enlightened sovereigns" and, as "enlightened legislators," they had the task of "enlightening the world"—was delusively simple.[39] Their doggedly reiterated strictures against the immorality and unlawfulness of "despotism" as such protested too much, for the contradictions which they built into their "sovereigns," "princes," and "legislators" betrayed their subscription to the tensile mentality of enlightened despotism, and their juxtaposition of positive and negative attitudes expressed not mere inconsistency, as is so often averred, but the degree of the tension.

For Helvétius, although despotism could not engender enlightenment and moral virtue, it was rooted in "everyone's desire to be a despot," which was in turn rooted in "the love of pleasure and hence in human nature itself."[40] For Mirabeau, this naturally rooted despotism was intolerable because it was part of a human contradiction: "The desire to be a despot is as natural to man associated in society as the hatred of despots is to him who has not been denatured by servitude." Man is both "naturally good and yet inclined to despotism," which "is the constant wish of humanity."[41] He then proceeded to add to the contradiction (while claiming to resolve it) by arguing against despotism as "unnatural," destructive of human rights, and yet also "diminutive of princes' power."[42]

For Holbach the tension was even greater, since he transvalued the political values: what invalidated despotism for him was not any ideal deficiency of system but only the actual deficiency of men. "Absolute power," he wrote in the context of demonstrating the moral purpose of government, "is very useful when it means to destroy abuses, abolish injustice, reprove vice, and reform morals. Despotism would be the best of governments if one could be promised that it would always be exercised by a Titus, a Trajan, or an Antoninus; but it usually falls into hands incapable of using it wisely."[43] It is Holbach, indeed, who affords the most striking example of the paradoxical sense behind the schematic notion of enlightened despotism. Because no single person could be trusted to withstand the temptations of power Holbach rejected "despotism" in every explicit mode — "Asiatic," "Western" (*Occidental*), "mitigated," and "legal" — but he acknowledged it in qualified form as the substructure of every system. "The law," he wrote, "ought to be despotic; but the sovereign should never be a despot."[44] By a curious reversal of traditional roles, the law is now to supply the power and the ruler is called upon to supply the knowledge.

The implications of this conjunction go far beyond the obvious sense of the frequently heard but isolated and undeveloped appreciations of a Voltaire, an Argenson, a Mercier, a Helvétius, a Grimm, a King Frederick for a "virtuous despotism" which imposes reform upon humanity "in spite of itself"[45] — visceral, impatient appreciations that are ubiquitous and timeless and have no pointed historical meaning. If we interpret Holbach's uncharacteristically laconic paradox in the light of Jeremy Bentham's corroborative focus on the law as primarily puissant command and of his affection for "the sovereign" — like, he enumerated, Catherine, Joseph, Frederick, Gustavus, and Leopold — as "a man of understanding" who must "prevail" over any "constitutional . . . obstacles . . . when he has the force of truth and power on his side," the invocation of the enlightened despot acquires a definite meaning for the age. What his most sophisticated modern commentator has frankly called the early Bentham's "admiration of 'benevolent despotism' " and " 'of enlightened despots' " was articulated *pari passu* with his effort to develop a new "logic of the [legislative] will" wherein the legislator spoke to the subject "from understanding to understanding."[46] At a time when the expanding possibilities of effective action were unsettling the familiar relationships — such as those between ruler and ruled, and between reason and will — which had constituted the intellectual landmarks of a world that had only to be stabilized, contemplated, and endured, the idea of enlightened despotism appeared as one of the myriad strange combinations devised to reassemble the detached elements. Eighteenth-century men tended to write "despotism" and "enlightened despots" rather than "enlightened despotism" precisely because some of them began to see in despotism a dissoluble system of exchangeable parts which would permit a novel and unsystematic association of personal understanding and impersonal power.

It cannot be emphasized too strongly that this schematic approach finds the historical meaning of enlightened despotism precisely in those qualities which have in the past sponsored the conviction of its historical absurdity — in its contradictions, in the infrequency with which the belief in it was espoused, and in the instability of the belief when it was espoused. For just these were the characteristic qualities of all political thinking in the eighteenth century, and just these are the characteristic qualities of political thinking whenever resort is made to enlightened despotism. Recent studies have stressed the "ambivalence," the "complexity," and the "persistent oscillation" of eighteenth-century political theory between the poles of enlightened despotism and constitutional liberty, consonant with the uncertainty of intellectual reformers about the political means wherewith to institute economic, social, and legal change. These studies have stressed too the gradual emergence of a preference for anti-absolutist constitutional liberty, as disillusion with sovereigns — both with those who refused to be enlightened and with those who claimed with apparent hypocrisy to be — grew apace after 1770.[47] But behind the vacillating and temporary nature of the commitment to enlightened despotism was an attitude that impelled eighteenth-century men to recur to it as much as they did despite the prevailing intellectual doctrine in and around them and that would lead men to recur to it again and again, under analogous conditions, long after the eighteenth century had drawn to its close. There was much of the exigent and the impulsive in the attitude, but there also was a conviction of its rightness for the moment that invites further inquiry.

It behooves us, then, to understand what made enlightened despotism, in its broad figurative sense, a comprehensible opinion in its original, eighteenth-century phase. What made such an unlikely association as a lawfully unlimited sovereign with an authority powered by law both thinkable and persuasive to those who did think it and were persuaded by the possibility of it were the changes in the connecting devices, or conventions, which had traditionally convinced men of the effectiveness of the legal limits on sovereignty. By tracing the shifts in such intermediate conventions and uncovering what had to be done with the conjunctions of organic tradition in order to adapt them for similar service in a disorganized situation, we can gain access to the meaning of a schematic enlightened despotism that was so ambiguous in its overt eighteenth-century usage.

Cases in the theoretical rather than the practical conventions of enlightened despotism will be adduced here because the separation between the theory and practice of enlightened despotism which previous research has established as a crucial historical fact of the eighteenth century makes the separate treatment of either historiographically permissible; because the location of the literal lead-ins to "enlightened despotism" in the realm of theory makes its treatment historiographically convenient; because the demonstrable persistence of tradition in political language makes the confrontation of novelty in political theory historiographically transparent; and because the parallel tensions which have been established within both the theory and the practice of enlightened despotism and which raise the possibility of an isomorphic structural relationship between the two realms render the rational linkages of theory potentially luminescent of the more obscure combinations in practice and thus make the separate treatment of the theory historiographically valuable.

The Authoritative Connection   2

There are two comparative problems, affecting the relations
between the structures we associate with the seventeenth
century and those of the later eighteenth, which recapitulate
on the theoretical level general problems of enlightened
despotism as such. These are the problems, first, of the
comparative criteria of legitimacy in government and, second,
of the imperceptibly shifting connections between political and
constitutional thinking.

On the first score, just as there is a real question of whether
the enlightened despots brought changes of mere degree or of
essential kind to the work of their unenlightened predecessors,
so there is a real question of whether the natural-rights thinkers
of the later eighteenth century brought changes of mere degree
or of an essential kind to the work of their natural-law
predecessors. The intricacies of Robert Derathé's *Rousseau et
le science politique de son temps*[1] would have to be multiplied
exponentially to distinguish a less maverick and less anti-
absolutist philosophe from his theoretical forebears. For the
links running back through early eighteenth-century popular-

izers like Barbeyrac and Burlamaqui to the great pioneering theorists of the seventeenth century are palpable enough to suggest a hypothetical interpretation of enlightened despotism as a case of "theoretical lag"—as a case, that is, of men attacking eighteenth-century political issues with seventeenth-century ideas.

The second comparative problem surfaced in late eighteenth-century theory through the juxtaposition in the same theorists of commitments, apparently contradictory in terms of seventeenth-century thinking, to both absolute and constitutional government—a change all the more revealing for being unremarked by those who registered it. The juxtaposition has shown itself to be but imperfectly rationalizable by being stretched along the means-to-end axis so often employed to explain inconsistencies in political theory. It is, indeed, precisely insofar as the relationship between absolutism and constitutionalism is not rationalizable along this axis that the problem becomes one appropriate to the asymmetrical schema of enlightened or legal despotism rather than to the congruent category of an enlightened or constitutional absolutism.

The fact is that not only did different figures—equally representative for our problem—split on whether absolutism or constitutionalism was the ideal end ("liberal" Physiocrats inclined to absolutism and authoritarian Cameralists to constitutionalism—a constellation itself an indication of paradox), but for others, such as Voltaire or Montesquieu, who committed themselves to both absolute and constitutional monarchy with apparently equal finality at different times, a possible relationship of ends and means did not even arise. Finally, Kant climaxed the problem toward the end of the century by fusing the contradictions and committing himself to an autocratically ruled representative constitution which would itself be both a final end of nature and a means to the moral freedom of man.[2]

At stake, in this question of an absolutism and a constitutionalism considered both as complements and as opposites, is the capacity of the theoretical schema of enlightened despotism to illuminate the proportions of political support and resistance in the attitude of corporations, of bureaucrats, and of individualists to the state. These proportions have continued to be puzzling in themselves because the external continuity of these groups from the seventeenth century, their shifting relations with one another, and their rhetorical subservience to monarchy permitted them little authentic theoretical expression of their actual positions in the eighteenth century.

If we can resolve these two problems of theory—that is, if we can explain how the unobtrusive changes in the seventeenth-century natural-law assumptions made what seems ambiguous in the enlightened despotism of eighteenth-century men unambiguous to them and how the distinctive relationship of absolutism and constitutionalism in the eighteenth century required some such concept of enlightened despotism, or a political cognate, then we shall have taken the blatant self-contradiction out of the concept. And perhaps we can illuminate, if not resolve, the two parallel problems of historical practice—the relationship between the policies of pre-enlightened and enlightened autocrats and the paradox of enlightened limits and despotic extension in the actual record of enlightened despotism.

For the first of these theoretical problems—the relationship of seventeenth-century natural-law to eighteenth-century natural-rights principles of political legitimacy—the solution which is relevant to the intelligibility of enlightened despotism is located in the connective device fashioned by flexing the idea of authority. The decisive intellectual change which explains what theory there was of enlightened despotism in the second half of the eighteenth century, we are often told, is the change from the static, orderly, security state of seventeenth-century natural law to the active, reforming, welfare state of later eighteenth-century political and social thought. Now the force of this shift from the safety principle to the welfare principle is undeniable, and the prominence of Physiocrats and Cameralists in the literature most relevant to the problem of enlightened despotism testifies to the particular susceptibility of

human welfare—usually identified with the newly emphasized right of earthly happiness, measured by pleasure and
property—to sovereign promotion.[3] In the well-known Physiocratic terms: "Men, by joining in society, have no other object
than to institute among themselves the rights of common and
private properties with which to procure the whole sum of
happiness and enjoyments possible for humanity. . . . Whoever
exercises the tutelary authority holds the happiness of man in
his hands."[4]

Whatever the differences between the Physiocrats and the
Cameralists (the later generation of this long-lived school
headed by J. H. von Justi and Josef von Sonnenfels) on the score
of economic policy, they shared a similar point of view and
analogous quotable propositions on the humanitarian welfare
principle. Thus in the oft-cited Cameralist terms: "The substance of all duties of the ruler . . . is to make his people
happy . . . , and he must apply all appropriate means and
regulations to this end." "Since the supreme power now
combines in itself the community will, its prerogative is likewise
to determine how the community energies shall best be used for
the common welfare." "We cannot keep ourselves from looking
to the head [*Oberhaupt*] of a society. It is a result of the
attraction which simplicity and unity have for us, and these in
turn are the symbols of order and truth; it is the precious
assertion of our reason, through which we deliberately subject
ourselves, despite our inclination to independence, for our own
welfare and from our love of order. . . . We perceive society,
and we perceive ourselves as part of society, in the prince, in
this permanent oracle of the general reason; he is its symbol, its
image, the representation of it that commands reverence. . . .
In monarchy the citizen sees the center of power, unified in the
One, as the center of welfare. . . . Subjects are willing enough to
borrow the criterion of their happiness from the criterion of the
power to do good which they ascribe to their prince."[5]

And yet there are several difficulties in the argument that the
new concern with increasing the material welfare of individuals
provides *as such* the rationale for the combination of monarch-

ical reform and extended powers that we call enlightened despotism. In the first place, seventeenth- and early eighteenth-century natural-law thinkers assigned to the state not only the preservation of external order but also the conditions for the moral "virtue" or "perfection" — to use the terminology of Spinoza and Leibniz, respectively — of its citizens, and it is hard to see why the definite mission of increasing earthly happiness should require more despotism than the indefinite mission of mending the ways of man to man.

Second, the idea of happiness was itself ambiguous, since men felt both that it was capable of management by political means and that it was ultimately attainable only by individuals. Aside from sovereign action in removing obstacles — and however convenient for historians if this had been the epitome of enlightened despotism, most formulations of the theory envisaged positive action far beyond such removal[6] — the focus on happiness simply relocated the problem of explaining the compatibility of the liberty and the authority in enlightened despotism from general policy to economic policy.

The third reason for doubting the expanding-welfare thesis as the explanation of enlightened despotism is that it ignores the considerable number of eighteenth-century theorists, exemplified by Frederick the Great and Kant, who were members of the central European kind of state to which enlightened despotism was especially appropriate and who yet carried on the modified version of what we may call Hobbes's day-and-night-watchman state, either disregarding or redefining the happiness principle.[7]

For these reasons — because the expanding-welfare thesis repeats rather than explains the combination of enlightened individualism and political authoritarianism and because its range is so narrow — the historical distinctiveness of the theories that argued the essential complementarity of unlimited monarchy and individual rights in the second half of the eighteenth century stemmed not from the new attention being paid individual and social happiness as such, but from a more fundamental novelty underlying it as a public issue. This fundamental novelty was a change in the conception of authority which categorically differentiated the authority that was grounded in seventeenth-century natural law from the authority that made possible the liberal, or enlightened, despotism of the later eighteenth century.

The authority in seventeenth-century theory was primarily an authority of origins. This ground of legitimacy was patent in the accepted species of what Hobbes called "natural government": both the "paternal" and the "despotical" types of kingdoms were validated by a derivative "right of dominion," one stemming from generation and the other from conquest.[8] Nor was the validation etiologically different in the more regular case of political institution, despite the apparent role assigned to contractual ends. For the power of the ruler was a function of his authority, and this authority was a formal consignment by the community, every member of which — in Hobbes's terminology — "*shall authorise*" all the actions and judgments of the sovereign; from this authorization "are derived all the *rights*, and *faculties*" of the sovereign.[9] This conferred authority was thus differentiated from the ruler's power, which was a mere means derived from the authority to serve the purpose of the authority. The ruler's power to realize the ends of the civil society was not a direct delegation from the community but rather depended for its very existence upon an authority sanctified by its origins in the natural rights of man. It was precisely because natural rights were alchemized into political authority before they could sponsor political power that the derived authority of the ruler was more binding than the ends to which he put his power and that the community could not, as a matter of right, claim a share in the sovereign power or normally recover it in case of its abuse. Hence the famous Hobbesian disjunction that "in constituted states . . . it is authority, not truth, that makes the law" was designed to exclude any consideration but that of origins from the idea of effective authority.[10]

This seventeenth-century idea of a politically a priori authority was predicated on a world view which postulated a continuum in the organization of all things, linking the original

structure of the cosmos, including its human nature, without
essential gap or resistance, to all the knowable phenomena of
nature and activities of man.[11] But by the second half of the
eighteenth century this general assumption, and particularly its
corollary of an independent authority of origins, mediatory
between the original rights of the community and its invariable
obedience to the power of the ruler, was fretted away, torn apart
by the growing general stresses upon the relations between uniform principles and multiform facts and by the particular
strains between the emphasis on human rights and the emphasis
on sovereign power. In such standard liberal formulations as
Diderot's article on political authority in the *Encyclopédie*,
authority was either a matter of right when it was in the people
or a title of power when it was transferred to the ruler; whether
political authority would be reconverted into popular right
depended entirely on the nature of the end to which the ruler
used his power. "The prince has from his subjects themselves
the authority [*autorité*] he has over them. . . . The crown,
government and public authority are properties of which the
body of the nation is the owner and the princes are the
usufructuaries, the deputies, the trustees. . . . The end of all
government is the good of the governed society. . . . Each
society must establish sovereigns with sufficient power [*pouvoir*]
to achieve its objects. . . . Good princes know that they are
holders of power only for the happiness of the state."[12] In such
a standard authoritarian formulation as Frederick the Great's,
the brief discussion had more to do with origins of the prince's
power than of his authority, and the real ground of obedience
to the ruler, over and above coercive power, had to do with the
ends to which the power was put.[13]

By the middle of the eighteenth century, indeed, political
writers were explicitly spelling out, as *the* criterion of valid
government, the idea of an authority that was grounded in the
capacity of rulers to fulfill social purposes. Justi, magisterial
Cameralist by profession and loyal Prussian by adoption, stated
flatly: "The best government will ever be that which most
completely satisfies the final end for which men live in
commonwealths: all other conceptions which men have of a

good government are false and void.... No one can govern
rational and free beings except through the purpose of
promoting their welfare and making them happy."[14] Sonnenfels, equally Cameralist but more rigorously rationalist,
clarified a step further by insisting that in the Justian equation
of formal purpose and substantive happiness, it was rather the
category of purpose than the fact of happiness that was the
most fundamental basis of authority:

The promotion of general happiness is the object of all states,
to be sure, in the period of their origin, and it is their perpetual
aim; for that very reason, however, it cannot be taken ... as
the general fundamental, because by means of this fundamental the goodness of measures, which consists in their
harmony with the ultimate purpose, must be tested.... In
case, therefore, the promotion of the general happiness is
assumed as the chief fundamental principle, the decision will
amount to this: "It promotes the general happiness because it
promotes the general happiness."[15]

Sonnenfels's own "chief fundamental" was "the public welfare"—that is, "the security and comfort of life." In this
context, however, it was not the alternative content of the
purpose but the necessity of exalting the telic criterion into a
principle, for which he found the empirical notion of happiness
unfit, that was a primary concern for him and a revelation for
us.

   But it was Holbach, with his usual talent for blundering into
revelatory anomalies, who most transparently signalized the
new telic grounds of legitimacy by blithely mixing the motifs of
origins and ends in the revised idea of authority. "The citizen
obeys the law, the public will, the sovereign authority," he
wrote in definition of the "Source of authority," "only because
he hopes that they will guide him more surely toward durable
happiness than his own desires do."[16]

   The shift in political thinking from considerations of origins
to considerations of ends, from justification by cause to justifi-

cation by effect—a shift which underlay the more graduated expansion of the security function to include the welfare dimension—was a principled reorientation which betokened a changed attitude toward the whole realm of human relations. The change, which has been overdramatized by Foucault as the "mutation" wherein "history" replaced "order" as the primary "mode of being" in man's view of the world at the end of the eighteenth century,[17] should be modulated for its application to the period immediately preceding, the period most germane to our concerns here. Certainly enlightened despotism can hardly be understood without grasping the implications of the shift from an approach which posited a natural and social cosmos with a priori rational structures and consequent phenomenal expressions of or deviations from it to an approach which posited natural and social realms with an immanent and emergent rationality to be discovered and realized in phenomena operationally. But it can hardly be understood, either, without appreciating the inertia of political thinking which referred the new intellectual activity to the established political authority.

Hence the new emphasis upon the necessity of "enlightened"—in the sense of systematically trained and actively rationalizing—rulers. For Justi not only was it the function of the Cameral sciences to supply "rational grounds" for economic policy and not only were these sciences themselves "logically based upon the essence and nature of the state"—that is, upon the principle of common happiness which was the final purpose of the state—but "unlimited governments" could administer these sciences in the light of this principle by "subjecting their will to reason," which "stabilizes" [*festsetzt*] the will, prescribes the final purpose of the state as the supreme principle of action, and insures consistency in the choice of means.[18] Hence the ruler must keep in mind not "this or that part of the ultimate purpose but the purpose in its whole inner coherence [*Zusammenhang*]," and his duty therefore is both "to enlighten and to direct the united will of the people—that is, its will to happiness."[19]

Sonnenfels was even more pointed in his assertion of universal principle as the logical foundation of the ruler's policies: "The mere empiricist in politics is as little to be regarded as a statesman as the empiricist in the healing art is to be regarded as a physician."[20] Clearly, the rational structure which seventeenth-century publicists had built into the constitution of the sovereign office, leaving rulers with the responsibility merely of moral fidelity to the original conditions of the office, was by the later eighteenth century relocated and made dependent upon the character and policies of the rulers themselves.

The mental shift to the telic view of politics was such as to overshadow the older genetic view but not to eviscerate it. The frequent admixture of appeals to the traditional virtues of benevolent royal paternalism with the newfangled requirement of royal perception of social ends exemplified the accretive character of the change, and the indiscriminate synonymity of "benevolent" and "enlightened" despotism is its lasting testament. The overlap of the two motifs, however unequal in composition and ambiguous in consequence, yielded a characteristic syndrome, and it was this syndrome that both produced the literal doctrine of "enlightened" or "legal" despotism and itself manifested the more indefinite political mentality most suitably described by that schema.

The combination of constituent contract and consent, on the one side, with the utilitarian purposes of the general happiness and welfare, on the other, became standard despite the demonstrations by Hume and Bentham of its artificiality and of its genetic invalidity. The upshot of the uneven combination was to make the independent authority of the government, addressed to social ends which only a rationally minded government could pursue, continuous with the derivative authority of the ruler which was a function of the collective power mandated to him via contract by the community. Genetic legitimacy was assumed in any ruler who actually exercised public power (the tendency to define tyranny in terms of the abuse rather than the usurpation of power was an indication of the indifference to constitutent title)[21] over the security functions which had always been appropriate objects of the community's compelling will and which were explicit provisions of the constituent contract consented to by the community. The incremental authority over the welfare ends transcended the constituent power and enlightenment of the contractant community and therefore amounted to a "despotic" extension of the legitimate power precisely insofar as the ruler displayed an incremental enlightenment.

Thus the Physiocrats' literal theory of "legal despotism" joined both the Cameralists' analogous theory and the more diffused general attitude to politics by connecting the new independent authority over the flexible ends of the community with the old genetically defined authority to exercise legitimate power. The redefinition of "security" from the traditional maintenance, by force, of inner peace and outer defense to the newer rational consistency of the sovereign will was one modulation of the change. Sonnenfels's combination of security and comfort under welfare, like Condillac's and Montesquieu's insistence upon security as a necessary ingredient of the liberty which it was the business of the state to preserve and promote, was a striking example of the merger. In Condillac's terms: "When the sovereign disposes of nothing arbitrarily, people enjoy what they have with security. . . . As long as the sovereign power is not arbitrary, it does not need to use violence to command obedience. . . . It assures liberty, therefore, in the relationship the citizens have to it."[22]

The Physiocrats' literal theory of enlightened despotism spelled out this merger by distinguishing specifically between the sovereign's legitimate power and the additional authority he possessed insofar as he directed men to the realization of ends which only they could realize and which he could not compel. Thus Nicolas Baudeaux, in 1767, categorically distinguished "authority" from what he called "superior force," defining the former as "the capacity to secure the best possible execution of the natural law of justice and the natural order of universal beneficence." Of the three main functions of the sovereign — protection, administration, and education — he, like his mentor Quesnay, found the last, which instructed citizens in their rights and duties under the law and order of nature, to be the crucial aspect of the state's authority precisely because it directed men toward ultimate social goals which were beyond the range of the collective power to reach.[23]

The ambiguity of enlightened despotism can be traced in good measure to the deposit of the two different ideas of authority — that is, of original coercive authority and of telic exemplary authority — in the same sovereign organ, and nowhere was this confusion so blatant as in that most explicit proponent of enlightened despotism, Mercier de la Rivière. By virtue of its origin in the collective will of the community, the sovereign "tutelary authority," as he called it, is characterized essentially by "the physical power to make itself obeyed," but it is by virtue of its function in realizing *l'évidence*, the self-evident truths of the natural order, that the "tutelary authority" becomes a legal despotism. For Mercier, legal despotism is based not so much on the authority of the laws themselves as on the authority of the reason behind the laws.[24] This conversion of reason from a function of freedom to a function of authority was the Physiocrats' means of equipping the unitary power of government to deal with the liberty of rational men, since the authority of reason requires the imperfect liberty of trust in those who do not yet understand it and is a way station to the perfect freedom of complete understanding. This increment of an authority that indefinitely transcends power, added to the definite authority that exercises power, shows how absolutism could take on the connotation of a despotism that was yet respectful of liberty. It was an early theory of what has since become a familiar problem — a theory of how men can be forced to be free.

The idea of authority has a continuous history that reaches back to the ancient Romans: it has ever served to join coercive power and uncoercible direction under a single mantle of legitimacy.[25] Its invocation during the later eighteenth century undoubtedly supplied a measure of theoretical integrity to the idea of an enlightened despot. It was resorted to because extra-theoretical factors—that is, the historical fact of monarchical persistence over the centuries and the hoary belief in the capacity of personality to contain contradiction—made the enlightened despot the only possible, but still hardly conceivable, agent of such ill-assorted, cumulative governmental functions as the provision of compulsory safety for the community and the promotion of a prosperity self-sustained by its citizens.

If this flexible and precedented concept of authority provided the notion of enlightened despotism with an integrating bond of principle *between* its original orderly and its subsequent telic liberalizing functions, there remains the question of whether, behind the inevitable osmosis through the medium of authority which admitted coercion into the putatively uncoercible sphere of rational gratification, anything *within* the contemporary emancipatory end itself theoretically required an enlightened despot. Now plainly, such usual formulations of social ends as "political liberty," "the assurance of property, life, and liberty," and "the happiness of society" make no such requirement, since these ends are more appropriate to the constituent community, taken distributively or collectively, than to the unlimited sovereign thereof—for it was, after all, the community's liberty and happiness that were concerned and only it could realize either.[26] Those political writers who subscribed to this kind of formulation—and they were preeminent both in numbers and repute—either rejected enlightened despotism out of hand as incompatible with the welfare end, both in its individual and in its collectivist constructions (like Montesquieu and Diderot), or, like Helvétius, Holbach, and Raynal, advocated it sporadically on an ad hoc basis, to overcome initial inertia or to overcome the individual's or community's actual failure to fill its theoretical role.

But there was one conception of the liberal utilitarian end that did exclusively postulate enlightened despotism or a euphemistic cognate. This was the attribution to government of the one civil end that was necessarily and equally beyond the reach of the individual citizen and the community alike—to wit, the regulation of the disharmonious relations between the individual and the community. The most explicit formulation of this distinctive sovereign function was Justi's, for he drew a precise distinction between "the happiness of the whole society," which is "the collective best" as such, and "the common happiness," which is the political sovereign's reconciliation of the individual with the collective happiness: "The final purpose of instituting a state is the common happiness, or the union of the welfare of every member of the civil society with the collective best." "In all the affairs of the country, the attempt must be made to put the welfare of the separate families in the most accurate combination and interdependence with the collective best, or the happiness of the whole state."[27]

The Physiocrats' conception of this political end which was singularly appropriate to an enlightened despot, by the essential default of the individual and the society as interested parties, was more implicit but equally definite. For both Quesnay and Dupont de Nemours, only the sovereign "tutelary authority"—"enlightened by the flame of reason . . . and knowledgeable through reason"—could teach and enforce the natural laws which regulated the natural rights of individuals in conformity with the natural order of things because both the individual and the society made up parts of the situation to be regulated. The individual looks to the exercise of his natural right, that is, "the right that man has to the things suitable for his enjoyment"; society represents the natural order, but in a form potentially destructive of the property which is the primary object of individual natural right—a potentiality essentially conditioned by the inherent inequality among men in their capacity to enjoy natural rights; only the "tutelary authority" or "tutelary sovereign," then, applies natural laws in a way that at once "expands rather than restricts men's use of their natural right" and guides its exercise in accordance with the "rule" constituting the beneficent "physical and moral order of nature."[28]

We may infer, from such definite exemplars, an attitude contributory to the meaning of more indefinite cases. The mentality favorable to the schema of enlightened despotism came into play whenever the welfare of the individual citizen was acknowledged as a discernible factor in the general welfare and an awareness of class, party, or status divisions inhibited the community's capacity to define the general welfare in a way that would be both compatible with individual rights and harmonious with the collective interests of the society. Then independent sovereign rulers tended to be assigned an authority far beyond their traditional constituent powers, to entitle them to procure "the benefits which," in Holbach's words, "their talents, their solicitude, and their virtues increase for their countries" and on which the entire legitimacy of the rulers "is founded."[29]

The Constitutional Increment 3

A second connective device that made the apparent paradox of
a schematic enlightened despotism — whatever the terminology
in which it was actually couched — generally conceivable and
fitfully desirable was the novel relationship which was established between absolutism and constitutionalism as substantive
kinds of government. It is true of course, as has been previously
remarked, that the opposition which we expect from the
confrontation of absolutist and constitutional systems was
minimized by the common indifference of eighteenth-century
publicists to questions of political structure because of their
overweening concern with beneficent governmental results
from any kind of political structure. Negative confirmation of
the correlation between such structural disinterest and the
recourse to enlightened despotism can be seen in the growing
overt challenge to absolute rule in any form — whether despotic, enlightened, or both — which accompanied the revival of
interest in political structure after the climactic conjuncture of
British Commonwealth radicalism, the American Revolution,
and the Turgot ministry in the mid-seventies.[1]

But if as a matter of historical fact the significance of the issue of absolute versus constitutional political structure varied inversely with the advocacy (whether explicit or postulated) of enlightened despotism, as a matter of historiographical perception the issue was continuously significant for the understanding of the mentality behind the advocacy of enlightened despotism. In the usual manner of historiographical reciprocity, moreover, the issue itself may then be illuminated by that mentality. For the same kind of thinking that explains the resort to enlightened despotism helps to explain the reconciliation of absolutism and constitutionalism for those to whom the question of political structure did come to seem essential. And the mode of this reconciliation, in turn, was often predicated on the assumption of an enlightened despotism that was overtly denied.

There were, in general, two levels of linkage between absolutism and constitutionalism for those who at one time or another advanced theoretical positions favorable to enlightened despotism. First, a whole series of ad hoc relations between absolutism and constitutionalism, appropriate to the stage of loose and nonchalant political thinking about such structural issues, served the purpose of neutralizing the genetic distinction between limited and unlimited government in the service of their compatible contribution to the socially beneficent ends of government. Several of these devices on the level of tactical theory are familiar from another perspective, as so many pieces of evidence against the theoretical integrity of enlightened despotism; but they assume a different aspect when they are viewed as reconciliatory devices which establish a positive, if conditioned, function for enlightened despotism, suspending the invalid connotations of the despotism, establishing its innocence by external association with constitutionalism, and normalizing the enlightened species of despotism as the necessary counterbalance of constitutionalism.

The first of these ad hoc devices was the resort to a kind of specialization of function between enlightened despotism and constitutionalism whereby each was valid in its own way, together constituting the complete government and thus complementing rather than confronting each other. The most obvious and frequent application of this device was made by the many publicists who allocated enlightened despotism to hyphenated political theory and constitutionalism to generic political theory—that is, who favored or assumed a provident authoritarianism for specific fields of public policy and argued for representative constitutions in their generic theories of politics. This division of theoretical labor is well known in the case of the Physiocrats, whose appeal to "legal despotism" or its equivalent, "tutelary authority," in economic policy was balanced by Turgot's project of a representative constitution for France, a project appropriate to the long-range Physiocratic vision of a liberated society of free property-owners.

But the device held as well for Cameralists, who had no such peculiar vision, and indeed, far beyond the particular orbit of economics, for the generality of publicists who concerned themselves with specialized applications as well as with general principles of politics. Thus the same Justi who in his Cameralist disquisitions on administrative science focused upon "the monarch's monopoly of government" as the primary feature of the governmental "structure" (*Beschaffenheit*) which produced "true power" in the state and especially upon "the German princes' exclusive possession of supreme power in their particular states" argued in his general treatise on political philosophy for "mixed government . . . in which the supreme power is divided . . . and the separate branches of the supreme power are placed in proper balance with one another" as "the best form of government" by the criterion of "the fundamental constitution of the state." A. L. von Schlözer was both a political journalist and a proponent of statistics as well as a political theorist. As a political journalist he insisted that his mission was merely "to uncover abuses" and not either "to judge or to instruct" much less to criticize the princely governments of Germany, in contrast to his principled opposition to "oligarchy" and "ochlocracy." As a pioneer for the administrative science of statistics he defined "the general form of states" in fundamental authoritarian terms to be "the right as well as the power of the head (sovereign, ruler, *tyrannos* in ancient Greek) to issue irresistible commands . . . and physically to compel obedience," and in this context he stipulated "the formula comprising the essence of every state" similarly to read "power, unity, and administration." But as a political theorist he expressly rejected Pope's maxim of indifference to forms of government, recommended mixed government on the principle that "every power must have its counter-power," and predicted "woe to the state . . . where there is no popular representation."[2]

The apparent vacillations of French radical publicists between enlightened despotism and constitutional liberty made similar sense in terms of a structural political differentiation that was independent of either the author's development or of the author's view of society's development. In the case of these publicists the differentiation was between the educative and the generic functions of government. Both Helvétius and Holbach invoked a self-determined sovereign power and even an occasional apology for despotism in the context of the state's responsibility for the moral training of its citizenry — that is, in *De l'esprit* and *Ethocratie* respectively — and stressed the constitutional limits upon sovereign power when they delivered themselves of general propositions upon the nature of political man — in *De l'homme* and *La politique naturelle* respectively. Raynal's argument in favor of enlightened despotism was ostensibly limited to the stage of primitive society, but he couched it in the context of a political pedagogy with far wider implications. "In its end and object politics resembles the education of youth. Both tend to form men. Their means should be similar in many respects. Like small children, when uncivilized peoples unite in society they want to be led by kindness and controlled by force." His diatribes against despotisms of all kinds, including the enlightened variety, were placed, on the contrary, in the context of his conclusive disquisition on government in general.[3]

A second way of making ad hoc connections between

absolutism and constitutionalism — ad hoc in the sense that they provided an external compatibility rather than an internal consistency — was to think of one form in short-run terms and the other in long-run terms. In its simplest versions this device included the many recommendations of autocratic initiative for reforms requiring the violation of recalcitrant customary rights that were made by men who otherwise preached defense against the abuse of autocratic power — recommendations that have earned for eighteenth-century political writers their reputation for hypocrisy or, at best, for incoherence in their endorsing enlightened despots while rejecting enlightened despotism. But there were at least two kinds of substantive principles which were identified with the short-run and the long-run respectively, over and above the usual inadvertent distribution between short-term despotic reform and long-term constitutional guarantees, and which provided at least a psychological coherence between them.

For some political writers short-term and long-term were connected along a temporal line in an implicit relationship of cause and effect. Such a relationship was uncertainly implied in progressive formulations such as Kant's, which made an age of enlightenment under an enlightened prince preliminary to the realization of a representative constitution in an enlightened age. Kant charged this realization to the unspecified powers of the enlightened prince: toward it "the ambitions of sovereigns and their agents" should be directed and for it "a coherent education pursuant to a deliberate and purposeful plan of the supreme power in the state" should be imposed as a necessary precondition.[4]

This cause-and-effect relationship was certainly implied in educational formulations like Holbach's, whose "good king," or "enlightened sovereign," should not only "work for the present happiness of his subjects" as the one power capable of "reforming morals" but also "assure this happiness for the future . . . by binding his descendants with laws so connected with the state constitution that they cannot be violated or destroyed."[5] More transparent was the generative continuity of short-term and long-term as stages of a single process in the Physiocratic formulation of G. F. Le Trosne: "If absolute authority is necessary to overcome resistance and carry through a great revolution or a general reform . . . it makes permanent the plan it has executed only by binding itself, and then by discarding the fatal power to destroy its own work and by consolidating this work through institutions appropriate to maintaining it."[6] But most revealing of all, because it did not shrink from either the literal reference to "despotism" or the dialectical logic of appealing to a force for the production of its opposite, was Beccaria's utilitarian scheme: "A republic grown too vast can escape despotism [*dispotismo*] only by subdividing and then reuniting itself as a number of federated little republics. But how is this to be realized? By a despotic dictator [*dittatore dispotico*] with the courage of Sulla and as much genius for building up as he had for destroying."[7] In general, when the emphasis was on the *activity* of government, its unconditioned power was brought to the fore; when the emphasis was on the *being* of government, it was defined in terms of its constitutional structure.

Overlapping this cause-and-effect species but distinct in principle from it was an atemporal variant of the short-term–long-term connection: it posited synchronic relations between transient actuality and constant ideal which made them complementary theoretical components of a single reality rather than antagonists in the conflict between practice and theory. What distinguished this theoretical connection between actuality and idea from either a cause-and-effect or a means-end relationship was its reversibility: for different writers, or for the same writer in different contexts, either absolutism or constitutionalism could define the ideal toward which men must ever strive, with its alternate acknowledged as the ineluctable actuality with which men must contend at every moment in the foreseeable future. Thus, paradoxically, for the "liberal" Physiocrat Nicolas Baudeaux "true theocracy, which I call economic monarchy," was "an absolute perfection, . . . an ideal metaphysical point which reason conceives," while the hundreds of existing "mixed states" are derogations from this idea of a "unique and supreme will" which is "the wish of nature, the order of Heaven . . ."; while for the "absolutist" Cameralist J. H. von Justi, the "ideal state," "a kind of Platonic Republic," turned out to be a mixed government of balanced aristocracy and democracy, since this was the only form that could in theory redress the common tendency of actual governments to "abuse their power."[8]

In part, the allocation depended on whose actual selfishness, power, lust, and general propensity for evil were in view: when it was everyman's, then the saving power of the ruler marked the ideal state; when it was the ruler's, then constitutional balance of powers marked the ideal state. The well-known vacillations of such notables as Helvétius, Holbach, and Schlözer between the ideal of enlightened despotism and the ideal of constitutional liberty stemmed in good measure from the shifting perspectives whereby they tailored their ideal, sometimes to their judgment that actually "the greater part of mankind is stupid or wicked," and sometimes to the equally firm judgment that "rulers are men, and . . . a man who has power misuses it."[9] Kant's stereoptic recognition that "man is an animal which . . . requires a master . . . — but then the master is himself an animal, and needs a master" analogously helps to account for his tergiversations between the *deus ex machina* of "wisdom from above" and "the perfect civil constitution" which is Nature's highest end.

But it is precisely Kant's case which indicates that bi-directional pessimism was not the sole, or even the main link between actual politics and the ideal constitution. For through his cryptic political formulations we can glimpse the painful but strenuous effort of his generation to make intelligible the relationship between ideal and phenomenal worlds whose essential incongruity was their ineluctable point of departure. When so rigorous a thinker as he deliberately commingled the "form of government" (*Regierungsform*), which had necessarily to be a "republican [*representative*] constitution" (or be an *Unform*), with the "mode of government" (*Regierungsart*), which permitted formally unconstitutional monarchy "in the spirit of a representative system," for the purpose of giving himself the theoretical possibility of recommending governments "to govern autocratically and yet also to administer constitutionally [*autokratisch herrschen und dabei doch republikanisch . . . regiern*]," the desperation of the striving to find some point of political union between "the idea of human right" and the actuality of "human morals" comes across with special transparency.[10]

But the more physically minded intellectuals within the Enlightenment could not use the organic analogy and the regulative principle that permitted Kantian opposites to converge. For them a mechanical device of accommodation was available in the spectrum from actuality to ideality most candidly laid out by Justi, who juxtaposed autocracy in the concrete operations of government, a constitutional mixture of monarchy and democracy in the prudential structure of the state, and a constitutional blend of aristocracy and democracy in his ideal commonwealth. Others were not so explicit in their mediation, but the relating of actuality and ideality as elements of a plenitude rather than of an antithesis was characteristic of all those who longed for harmony and had to live with dissonance.

What rendered these contrivances intellectually satisfying was the existence, upon a more fundamental level, of an internal relation between absolutism and constitutionalism, a relation which exercised a subliminally convergent pressure upon the overt ad hoc devices. During the eighteenth century, and in response to distinctive intellectual and material conditions of governing in that age, the relationship between absolutism and constitutionalism was revised from its traditional status as the alternate determination of unlimited or limited government in the constituent fundamental law to a novel logical connection in which constitutions entailed the concentration and enhancement of absolute political power.

Instrumental in this revision was a new development in the meaning of constitution. The revised meaning, which extended rather than superseded the traditional sense of the concept, reflected a changed attitude toward the organs whose relations made up the substance of the idea of constitution, but just as important was the change the new meaning effected in the relations between the political and the constitutional theory through which these organs were approached. For through this change in the forms of thinking about government the concept of constitution became versatile enough to serve as the adjectival equivalent of enlightened in the theory of enlightened despotism.

Political theory had traditionally — at least since Bodin and Althusius — been assigned the ascertainment and analysis of norms and principles; to constitutional theory had gone the derivative task of describing the practical relations of existing organs in the light of these principles or the subordinate task of describing the actual joint history of these organs. Under this theoretical dispensation all legitimate polities, absolute and mixed alike, had constitutions — thereby excluding despotic government from polity and political theory — and the issue of unlimited versus limited forms of government was a practical choice between more or less preferable constitutional alternatives equally grounded in history.

But during the eighteenth century the genres tended to cross. Politics developed a theoretical literature devoted to the practice of government in accordance with the rules of prudence. From historic corporate constitutions there grew a normative theory of constitutional first principles, stipulating the representative ideal to be the essential feature of constitutions as such: as both Kant and Paine would categorically hold, constitutions had to be representative or they were not constitutions at all. Because these developments loosened rather than supplanted the traditional relations between political and constitutional theory the ideas of absolute and limited government were detached from their familiar conditioning assumptions and became susceptible to irregular combination, such as old-style corporations with new-style practical politics and old-style autocratic institutions with a new-style constitutional ethos.

The second of these irregular combinations — our concern

here—was made conceivable by the historical ambiguity of eighteenth-century constitutionalism whereby the formal constitutional warrant of traditional absolutism could modulate into the substantive constitutional norm of the representative system and convert the limiting conditions of the former into an extended function in the service of the latter. It was this transformation of a constitutional definition into a political increment that made the irregular idea of enlightened despotism a theoretical possibility.

What we need, to understand this intellectual operation, is to see how absolutist theory could use constitutionalism as a lever to despotism. For this we clearly need a more historical formulation of the problem than our own categorical antithesis of absolutism and constitutionalism, and we also need—just as definitely if not so clearly—a more problematic answer than the *thèse royale*, which, like the opposing *thèse nobiliaire*, defined the competence of its protagonist in the structurally congruent terms of historic constitutionalism. Indeed, just as the theoretical advocacy of enlightened aristocracy can only be grasped from the mediation of traditional hierarchy through constitutional liberalism into natural-rights sovereignty, the schema of enlightened monarchy can only be comprehended through the paradoxical escalation of absolutism through an infusion of modern liberal idealism to a constitutional despotism. To get at the process of this escalation, we must start from the plurality of meanings which "constitution" had in eighteenth-century usage.

Certainly the idea of constitution in the eighteenth century can no more be known from the exegesis of the term than can any other crucial political concept of the period, and what *we* mean to indicate by the idea—the body of operational principles governing the relations of organs within a political system—could be called "fundamental law" (especially in France) and "natural law" or "public law" or "elements of jurisprudence" (especially in Germany) as well as "constitution" (especially in Britain). Still the latter term was current in the political and juristic literatures of all these nations, and in each of them the range of references denoted by the same word exhibits the tendency of eighteenth-century men to see continuity where we see distinction and furnishes a substantive clue to the paradoxical invocation of constitutionalism for the unprecedented intensification of sovereign authority. For "constitution" retained its original Roman-law sense of any edict, ordinance, or law enacted by the sovereign ("anything it pleases the prince to order," in the crisp phrase of the *Encyclopédie*).[11] The term also retained its even more ancient Aristotelian sense of the permanent laws, institutions, and principles which composed the real framework of each regime. And the same term came to cover, in a sense achieving currency only during this very period, a prescriptive form of government, assigning various functions to various organs in a system of divided powers validated by the criterion of normative principle. The inclusion of the first two connotations in the same term had long reflected the resolution which was usually given to the problem of the absolute sovereign's superiority or subjection to the law: the linguistic homogeneity of fundamental law and sovereign enactment indicated their essential continuity as form and self-realizing actuality in the definition of any government. What was novel in the eighteenth century was the extension of this linguistic bond between actual power and genetic disposition to the theoretical doctrine of how this power should be organized. Just as the dovetailing of genetic and telic authority made up the principle of enlightened despotism, so did the overlap of the sundry meanings of constitution define its structure. The structure of enlightened despotism becomes comprehensible, indeed, as the juncture of the traditional descriptive with the incipient prescriptive theories of constitution.

The theory of absolutist constitutions in the traditional sense of constitution acknowledged supreme and indivisible power in the ruler and a countervailing power in no other governmental organ; but it acknowledged too, as necessary circumscriptions of the ruler's power, the fundamental laws which defined his office and the subordinate agencies through which all his powers were exercised upon his subjects. The laws which defined the absolute monarchy, and the agencies through which it communicated with the society at large, were traditionally conceived to be the natural laws of hierarchical order, the customary laws, and the intermediate magistracies appropriate to a corporate society.

The pattern of this traditional absolutist theory, which thus associated the political self-limitation of absolute power by the same divine and natural law that authorized it with the constitutional self-limitation of this absolute power by the same social agencies that transmitted it, goes back at least to Bodin, with his doctrine of a politically absolute monarchy governing through a constitutional "harmony" of estates, and persisted well into the eighteenth century. Its best-known formulation was Montesquieu's doctrine of the self-tempered monarchy, where "the prince is the source of all power" but yet is "limited by its very spring" and "governs by fundamental laws which necessarily supposed the intermediate channels [that is, 'the intermediate, subordinate, and dependent powers'] through which the power flows." Its broad diffusion can be seen in the Voltairean position which has been aptly called "constitutional absolutism," in the remonstrances of the *parlements* which claimed the harmony of their constitutional function with the principle of absolute monarchy, and in the German jurists who persisted in the effort to reconcile the absolutism of the princes with the constitution of the empire.[12]

But by the last third of the century three countervailing factors became so intrusive as to challenge the conventions which made this constitutional definition of political absolutism a plausible theoretical orientation. The political surge of the aristocracy undermined its constitutional position as a conduit of monarchical power; the emphasis on natural rights and individual utility undermined the natural definition of absolute political sovereignty; and the increase in the force available to the instrumentalities of the state dislocated the familiar balance between what was and what was not subject to political power. The theoretical impact of these revisionary factors could indeed be to produce the political theory of modern constitutionalism, which identified a representative constitution as the only valid principle of politics and placed it in fundamental opposition to absolutism. Many of the prominent figures of the late eighteenth century, as variegated as Diderot, Burke, and Paine, took this obvious course, which adumbrated one of the great confrontations of the nineteenth century.

Yet there was another option open, one that considered modern constitutionalism not as a political theory superseding the political theory of absolute sovereignty but as a constitutional theory homologous with traditional constitutionalism and affording an alternate way of organizing and articulating the constitutional structure of political absolutism. But like their opposite numbers—the partisans of traditional aristocracy or of the equally traditional mixed government who sought to update legal privilege by identifying it with modern constitutional liberty—the advocates of political absolutism altered the character of their politics with the change of constitutional associations. Absolute monarchy continued to be defined for eighteenth-century Europeans as the legitimacy of a single sovereign, unlimited by superior or equal human agency but definitely limited by those legal objectifications of his own power (both positive statute and subordinate agent) that actualized the fundamental laws of his own constitution. When these constitutional predicates of this political axiom were adapted to include the new constitutionalism, with its dislocation of the legal limit on sovereignty from the realm of actualizations to the realm of norms, absolute monarchy assumed an altered shape, at once more sharply delimited and more forcefully poised, for which enlightened despotism is not an inappropriate description. For paradoxically enough, the espousal of a constitutionalism which was designed ultimately to put human limits upon the sovereign power in the name of individual liberty had two immediate effects which turned external limits into internal instruments of heightened power. First, the theoretical shift from the graded emulsion of political and social authorities in an orderly continuum to the categorical differentiation between the spheres of political order and social liberty had the effect of turning the division between order and liberty into an incremental advantage for the monarchical organ which now possessed a constitutional monopoly of the ordering power. We may call this the shift in the axis of constitutional thinking. Second, the shift from institutional channels to constitutional norms turned the real conditioning of the sovereign power by its past into its potent knowledge for the future. We may call this the shift in the plane of constitutional thinking.

Those who shifted the axis of constitutional thinking retained the ideas of an absolute authority that is unlimited in its own sphere and of an absolute sphere that is defined by the law of its own constitution and by its characteristic mode of action. What they changed was the quality of the constitutional law and the line separating its mode of action from other modes of action.

Where the law had been special, moral, or conventional, assigning to the sovereign his own public sphere vis-à-vis the public functions of social and ecclesiastical institutions, the law was now general, natural, and rational, organizing government and individuals in a single order of natural society, complementary in their interests but separate in their functions. Government embodied the law in the law of nature; individuals embodied the rights which were ordered by the law. Within its own sphere, the sphere of the law in the natural law, government was thus unlimited in a novel infinite way, since its sphere was coextensive with the whole of the natural law and the power of its positive statutes enjoyed the same built-in unrestraint as the power of the natural laws that positively governed the actual course of nature. Such law was limited only by what it was not — that is, by the sphere of the individual rights protected by the natural law.

The characteristic mode of action of governments was the enforcement of the order in the natural order; the characteristic mode of action outside of government was the assertion of natural rights by individuals. Because the operative laws of nature were irresistible, so was the will of the sovereign in their service. Because these laws were uniform, so must the sovereign be unitary.

The second effect of the new constitutionalism in its monarchist version entailed the shift in the plane of constitutional thinking from the actual to the normative status of the defining limits on sovereign power. Like the turn of the axis, this shift in the plane of thought was predicated on the immediate relations which the structure of civil constitutions was now deemed to have with the structure of nature. Whereas civil constitutions had been traditionally descriptive of existing governmental structure and would later be prescriptive for the distribution of power within the state; and whereas the constitution of nature had been traditionally prescriptive of divinely authorized moral norms and would soon be deemed to be categorically distinct from the constitution of the state: at our eighteenth-century transfer point what was descriptive in the constitution of nature became prescriptive for the constitution of the state. The participation of representative bodies in government incorporated the link between the two constitutions, channeling the natural energies of men into the political reservoir of the ruler's authority and making a political requirement out of the natural distinction between what is and what is not amenable to collective control. Since representation, so conceived, was the institutional equivalent of the natural law that maximized the effective strength of the sovereign by fixing the appropriate boundaries and direction of political power, a modern representative constitution became, for those monarchical modernizers who conceived it so, the final mark of proper political organization by enlightened and aggressive absolute rulers. The conjunction of absolutism and constitutionalism becomes intelligible as a characteristic doctrine of moderate intellectuals who would have their king not only enlightened but — since they would commit him to action that would mutate the hybrid half-private, half-public property rights of churches and lay corporations in the old constitution — despotic as well.

The direct correspondence that the modernizers of absolutism thus established between the political order and the order of nature had the effect of making the political sovereign the natural spokesman for society and thus of bringing the sovereign as executor of natural order face to face with individuals as agents of natural rights, to the exclusion of the traditional intermediate authorities. For Quesnay, government was an extension of the natural order both because the correction for the individual's evil use of natural rights was built into the natural law itself and because government supplied men's reason with the "enlightenment" it needed to know the natural order.[13]

But it was Turgot who delivered what was perhaps the most impressive testimony of the intellectual process that could posit the change from the indefinite collaboration of all political and social authorities to the definite restraint of exclusive sovereign authority by individual right as a real extension of the public power, guaranteed no longer by an inscrutable divine decree but by the perceptible sanctions of nature. For Turgot enunciated the various elements in the change separately and problematically, and he made the connection without which their juxtaposition made no sense because he had to make it, without even knowing he was making it. Political authority, he wrote with deliberate incongruity, is to "repress independence without oppressing liberty," to "shackle men for their happiness."[14]

These formulations have meaning in the context of Turgot's belief that the sovereign's exclusive and indefinite power within the political sphere confronts only the rights of individuals outside the political sphere. The integrity of the sovereign's political sphere is guaranteed by its function—to "assure *the duration* of society's happiness," a function directly analogous to the constancy of nature's laws and directly counter to the variability of nonpolitical man in his history—and by the negative status of intermediate authorities, since "the restriction of the public welfare to a small number of men, . . . to the social class of which the legislators are part" is precisely the "fundamental vice" which must be rooted out by religion and proper government.[15] This alignment of a sovereign politics operating with the uniformity of natural law and confronting the fertile multiplicity of extrapolitical human rights furnished the rationale for Turgot's typical idea that the force of government varied directly with its respect for individual liberties. Only when government, he wrote, has a "religious respect for personal liberty, the freedom of labor, the inviolable conservation of property rights, and justice for all . . . can it be hoped that some day all the present chaos of politics will take a distinct form."[16]

Not unexpectedly, it was the same Turgot who exemplified most explicitly how the prescriptive mode of the new constitutionalism was conceived as an exponent of governmental power. His proposal for a hierarchy of representative assemblies from the village to the national levels was projected as an advisory council of individual property-owners which he considered to be included within the organization of the sovereign power, orienting it toward direct action upon individuals: it would "assure the royal power of commanding well"; it would have "no authority to oppose indispensable operations"; it would "increase tenfold the forces of the kingdom," specifically "by substituting a spirit of order and union for the spirit of disunion that increases tenfold the labors of Your Majesty and his servants and that necessarily and progressively diminishes Your Power"; in sum, it would "place the State in a complete, proportional, and visible harmony of interests with all the property-owners."[17]

But the fundamental grounds for Turgot's judgment that constitutional reform would bring a real increase of the monarchy's absolute power do not lie in these categorical declarations, which in any case, situated as they were in a memorandum of an incumbent controller-general to his king, have an inevitable bureaucratic flavor. The grounds for Turgot's judgment lay rather in his contextual notions about the relationship of constitutions to sovereign power, for in these notions lay the rationale which required that the mutation of traditional absolutism into an authority on a higher level of power, which some of Turgot's contemporaries (albeit not Turgot) called despotism, proceed necessarily through enlightenment. First, a constitution for Turgot was a constitution in the modern normative rather than in the traditional actual sense, and as such its institution was rather a command by sovereign power than a definition of that power. The trouble with France, he told the king, is precisely that "your nation has no constitution," and he recommended that his monarch have "the goodness" to give her one. This constitution, moreover, would be normative in that it must be addressed to rights founded "not on the history of men in society but on their nature," and for the installation of this just norm the king could "regard himself as an absolute legislator" in a new sense, unbound by historic rights and customary laws.[18]

The second of Turgot's crucial notions about this desirable constitution specified its affirmative function for sovereign power in terms of the enlightenment it guaranteed to this power. The role of the representative assemblies was specifically "to enlighten," and for Turgot this essential role worked in both of the directions crucial for politics: it served to enlighten the king and it helped the sovereign power enlighten the people. Thus the representative assemblies would "enlighten" the government "about the distribution of taxes and sectional needs," and the Council of National Education which Turgot projected as an integral part of the new constitution would instruct the nation in civics and thus make people "submissive to authority by reason rather than by fear."[19]

Perhaps most revealing of the assumptions behind this association of autocratic institutions with the new constitutionalism was Turgot's conviction, expressed on entirely different occasions and for both dimensions of the enlightening process, that the application of up-to-date knowledge by and to government was an essential condition of the despotic increment in sovereign power. Anent education by governments he was convinced that "despotic states" could last only when they duly indoctrinated their peoples, for "this power of education is one of the great principles in the durability of government."[20]

Anent the education of governors, equally, it was precisely for the unaccountable dimension of authority which transcended both the traditional law and the social contract that Turgot felt enlightenment in the governors to be indispensable. "Men are enlightened only by the lessons of experience," he generalized from his description of Lycurgus's constitution as a despotism which "submitted an entire nation of slaves to the cruelest tyranny," and he warned that legislators who ignore this rule "by perpetuating errors when they perpetuate their laws" provoke revolutions which "destroy the power which the laws draw from the sovereign authority and leave to them merely the authority which the laws draw from their own utility or conformity with natural equity."[21] The difference between an unacceptably and an acceptably authoritarian constitution obviously consisted for Turgot in the absence or presence of a continuing process of enlightenment.

And if this novel way of approaching constitutional problems in the second half of the eighteenth century helps to explain the anomalous combination of qualities that added up to express or tacit doctrines of enlightened despotism, it must be concluded too that these qualities help to explain some of the anomalies in the constitutional claims of the same period. Thus the influential Beccaria, whose treatise on crimes and punishments was devoted so prominently to limiting both the extensive and the intensive competence of the sovereign's right to penal legislation and who grounded this limitation so categorically on the fundamental contractual investment by men of "only the least possible portion" of their personal liberty in the politically relevant "deposit of public security," not only protested that "far from diminishing legitimate authority" his work "must serve to increase it" but was in fact assiduously courted by Frederick, Joseph, and Catherine — "enlightened despots" all, united at least in this admiration. Certainly relevant to this juxtaposition, and serving to make Beccaria's authoritarian claims something more than the usual cautionary rhetoric, was his peroration to enlightenment as the norm which would make the subject's liberty an increment of the sovereign's power. "To prevent the despotic spirit, which is in every man," he wrote, "from plunging the laws of society into its original chaos, . . . an enlightened man is the most precious gift the sovereign may bestow upon the nation and himself."[22] The conjunction sums up the constitutional thinking of an age.

Conclusion

Political Reality in an Active Key

The schema of enlightened despotism was thus made conceivable by two connecting devices — a functional criterion of
authority and a normative status for its constitutional structure — and we hereby confront finally within theory the
primordial question raised outside of theory by the dubious
reality of enlightened despotism in eighteenth-century political
practice: what kind of truth did the idea of enlightened
despotism have for those eighteenth-century writers who
explicitly accorded it any truth at all?

The categories of function and norm would seem to confirm
the familiar simple notion that whatever truth was vouchsafed
enlightened despotism in the eighteenth century was the truth
of an ideal, a kind of truth which, whether as a functional
Weberian ideal-type or a utopian vision of a normative
perfection, stood apart from the manifold concrete reality it
was to guide, reform, and harmonize. But in point of historical
fact the eighteenth-century view of the ideal was neither
Weberian nor utopian — at least not for enlightened despotism.
The ideal truth which was attributed to it was neither the truth

of a hermeneutic abstraction nor the truth of a higher reality. The truth of enlightened despotism was a truth of the actual world, of the same reality as the concrete manifold — but of this reality brought from a blur into focus. For the Physiocrat Baudeaux, the "true theocracy" which he preferred to call "economic monarchy" and we call "enlightened despotism" was "a being of reason" (*un être de raison*), at once "natural and essential."[1] Kant was even more explicit in asserting that unlimited sovereignty was rightly understood as the rational structure of actual political reality: the idea that every statute must be treated "as if it must come not from men but from some supreme and infallible legislator . . . expresses the following principle of practical reason — every actually existing legislative power is to be obeyed, whatever its origin."[2] For Physiocracy and for Kant alike, this intentional ambivalence of reason, manifesting both the structure of the actual world and its transcendence, was connected with the relationship which we have already seen them establish between nature and politics: what was descriptive in the laws of nature became prescriptive for the laws of the state.

Over and above the specific association with what was most flexible in the idea of reason, moreover, this way of thinking about enlightened despotism as a central reality vis-à-vis the off-center reality of everyday life was more generally articulated in a pervasive mode of eighteenth-century political language. Enlightened despotism or its political cognates were often to be found in the conditional mode, and this in contexts indicating that the conditional mode designated the intermediate status of a unifying reality inseparable from the facts of political life but yet existent on a different plane, operative at once behind and through them. When conceived in the conditional mode, enlightened despotism became a viable intersection of traditional theory and present needs; it became the expression of a political principle in the special language of political action.

With this correlation of the conditional mode and the active key we touch on a difficult theme that requires special discussion, for we abut here on the origins of a problem that would plague theorists throughout the nineteenth century and that remains troublesome to this very day: the problem of composing a language of action from linguistic components designed to communicate knowledge of the existing world. The approach to enlightened despotism through the conditional mode was an early case of what would become a standard device of the translation: the restatement of indicative assertions about reality as hypothetical conditions of action in such a way as to recast the real relations between fundamental principle and factual appearance into the practical relation of a fundamental quality to an existing agent who can realize himself only by acting in accordance with it. In this integral use of the conditional mode the whole of the indicated world, fact and principle alike, is transmuted into so many functions of the projected action: the definite subject becomes an open-ended agent and principles of reality become practical postulates. The connections between the indicated realm of knowledge and the conditional realm of action are delivered overtly by the factual existence of the agent and covertly by the subliminal continuities inherent in the terms and in the logic of the language employed to describe both realms.

In the instance of enlightened despotism, the principles which had been seen to underlie the fact of absolute monarchy were modulated into the active attributes of the ruler and the practical requirements of the regime — attributes and requirements which must be acted upon for absolute monarchy to become a fact at all. Enlightenment thus became the modern practical equivalent of old-style paternalism, and the despot the modern active equivalent of the old-style ordained autocrat.

Nowhere was this political function of the conditional mode more strikingly applied than in the surprising acceptance of a defense of despotism at the conclusion of Jaucourt's virulent diatribe against despotism in the *Encyclopédie*. Even if this coda be deemed a sop to the censor, the conditional form in which Jaucourt put it reveals how his mind worked when he sought to sublimate a fact of repressive despotism into a postulate of enlightened despotism. Within this conditional form—signified by the opening "it can be maintained that . . ."—Jaucourt developed an equally conditional content, making the traditional patriarchal ruler, whose actual despotic power was founded on the principle of benevolence, the politically logical antecedent of the contemporary despot, whose despotic powers are conditional on his governing in rational conformity to the law, thus converting the old foundation of paternalism into the modern postulate of enlightenment:

But it can be maintained that a king is master of the life and goods of his subjects because, loving them with a paternal love, he preserves them and cares for their goods like his own. Thus he acts *as if* all men were his own, taking an absolute power over all their possessions to protect and defend them. It is thus that, gaining the hearts and property of his people, he can declare himself master of them, although he actually never makes them give up their property save under the law.[3]

More usual but reflecting a similar orientation was the variant employed by Diderot, who came finally to reject enlightened despotism more literally than many others, but not before he had manifested the kind of thinking that led them to remain more persistently ambivalent about it. The context of Diderot's opposition to enlightened despotism as a matter of principle for its ultimate violation of human rights was his acknowledgment of its utter improbability as a matter of fact: the despot of an enlightened despotism must be "a good, resolute, just, and enlightened master," and when we "calculate the chances" of such an individual's actual existence we must conclude them to be minimal: "If these qualities taken separately are rare as they are, how much more so is their combination in a single man." But when Diderot was in his conditional posture his perspective was quite different. "*If* reason governed sovereigns . . . , peoples would not need to bind the hands of the sovereigns." Or, more explicitly, if we recall the terms attributed by Raynal to current opinion, "you will hear it said that the happiest government *would be* that of a just and enlightened despot." From this perspective the factual defections from enlightened despotism invalidate the constitutional alternative and, far from refuting enlightened despotism as such, validate it in its conditional mode. For since, as Diderot avowed in this mode, there are no popular restraints that cannot in fact "be broken or evaded" by the sovereign's lust for power — because "sovereigns have too great an advantage over peoples" — the government of sovereigns by reason expresses the only feasible, if hypothetical, rationale of power: for if, in Diderot's express citation of the old Tacitean saying, power is never stable enough when it is excessive, sovereignty is also never so powerful as when it "is compressed within limits."[4]

What was implied here by Diderot was explicit in others: behind this mode of thought lay the increasing recognition, as the century wore on, that despotism, whatever the name it went by and with all its antinomies of too much authority and too little power, was the primary indicative fact of political life, and that the despot, on condition of his enlightenment, was the only real agent who could connect this political life with the equally real order of nature. Rousseau was not alone in seeing men everywhere in chains. Mirabeau declared the desire for superiority and the correlative desire to abase others to be "the most active passions in the human heart," and he observed that the history of nations shows only "the names of conquerors and despots."[5] Asserting a limited monarchy to be impossible and monarchy itself to be "a perfect synonym for tyranny," Alfieri saw "in nearly all the countries of Europe only the figures of slaves, . . . universal servitude."[6] Alfieri insisted upon a republic as the only valid alternative to "tyranny," but his own denial of the possibility of a qualified despotism still furnished a negative proof of the kind of thinking that in others would produce an advocacy of enlightened despotism. For when he asked what action could be taken in a society of slaves to end the prevailing tyranny he could only suggest actions by "the tyrants themselves" — actions so unreasonable and violent that they would provoke the general republican will and opinion otherwise too weak and too uncertain to remedy anything.[7]

The positive side of this activist realism—that is, the readiness to make enlightened use of these ineluctable despotic agents—was articulated, consistently enough, by practical reformers like Sonnenfels and Pestalozzi, otherwise so diverse in interests and temperaments. Registering the actual stalemate of the available constitutional alternatives—the monarchy to which men are naturally attracted tends to abuse power and the mixed government which is recommended on the English model to check abuses of power tends to vacillation, faction, and turmoil—Sonnenfels demonstrated the function of the conditional mode in connecting traditional monarchy with present actuality. "If the subjects have given up the right to protect themselves," he asked, "what will prevent a monarch from misusing his power?" His reply: "A heart that loves its subjects and justice; the desire for true glory; the fear of the tormenting consciousness of having merited his subjects' curses; the trembling before the shame of future history."[8] In short, a benevolent and enlightened despot.

Even more striking, by reason of his nurture in the Swiss republic of Zurich and in the libertarian ideas of Rousseau, was the analogous tendency of J. H. Pestalozzi to slip into the hypothetical invocation of an open-ended monarchical power when he looked to the practical execution of his far-ranging project for "the satisfaction of our nature's fundamental needs" through the "enlightenment of all [the world's] peoples." "What, then, should be done?" he asked. His general answer was: "I imagine a sovereign whose legislation would conform with the fundamental needs of human nature." And his specification of this "sovereign": "I set my hopes on finding a king who is a friend of mankind and the father of his people. . . . It is a humiliating thought, but true: any advance in the good leadership of people must proceed from the cabinets of monarchs." Then Pestalozzi did proceed in fact to offer his services successively to those prominent enlightened despots, Joseph II and Leopold II of Austria.[9]

Thus there was a level in eighteenth-century thinking where enlightenment belonged with despotism as at once its necessary condition and its transcendent control. On this level enlightened despotism described political reality in words that had been devised to transmit knowledge of the existing world but that were now applied to convey the possibilities in this world for action to change it: the conditional mode marked the translation to this activist perspective. Hence it must be concluded that far from being negated, the status of enlightened despotism is defined both by its dubiety as an existing reality of eighteenth-century kingship and by its exclusion from the valid political doctrines literally asserted by any representative sample of eighteenth-century theorists. Like the state of nature, the social contract, and the general will, enlightened despotism existed neither as a general political fact that could be indicated nor as a logically necessary philosophical truth that could be demonstrated. Like them, it existed rather as an idea of reason—that is, as a conditional principle whose truth stemmed precisely from the hypothetical necessity of assuming it if any sense was to be made of a political existence that was contradictory in itself and of theoretical dualities unbridgeable in themselves. But enlightened despotism was both less and more than these concomitant ideas of reason. It was less because where they referred to universal human relations it referred to a particular political institution—the institution of monarchy—by whose peculiar characteristics it was inevitably shaped. It was more than the other ideas of reason because where they were congruent with the literal terms respectively defined by them it represented a whole way of thinking—for which there were several possible cognates—about a stable political reality that comprehended conscious possibilities of change and that was therefore both what it was and what it might be.

If this be contradiction let us remember, before we deprecate, that it was a historically representative contradiction. The popular culture of the eighteenth century was an anomalous polymorph of a preponderant commitment to tradition indeterminately modified by infusions of critical innovation.[10] The theorists of enlightened despotism, precisely because of their deliberate confusion of benevolent paternalism and legitimate absolutism with enlightened despotism, were closer to the attitudes of the inarticulate reading public than were the constitutional liberals among their intellectual colleagues, however more characteristic of the intellectual estate those liberals may have been. In the sociology of culture, the proponents of enlightened despotism may indeed be accorded a mediatory role between the collective mentality of the mass and the high culture of the philosophes.

And let us remember too that the contradiction between the definite results that are expected from political power and the indefinite force that is bestowed on political power is one that we have ourselves not resolved. Eighteenth-century men may not have practiced the enlightened despotism that some of them preached, but many of us still practice an enlightened despotism that we have not the honesty to preach. The theoretical parallel with what we do when we are in this dependent posture can be found in the eighteenth-century schema of enlightened despotism. Then, for the first time, was articulated the third of the three dimensions of political reality that have been with us ever since. In addition to the way this world looks when it is contemplated and the way this world looks to one who is preparing to act upon it, there is the most common perspective of all: the way political reality looks when we perceive it to be actionable—by somebody else. Small wonder that we have patented the eighteenth-century invention of enlightened despotism.

For the unfortunate fact of the matter is that we *have* had despots since the eighteenth century—rulers who brook no limit, save of their own devising, upon measures covered by the national security and the general welfare, and who brook no definition, even of their own devising, of the national security and the general welfare. Whether fortunate or unfortunate, the concomitant fact is that since the eighteenth century all despots, whatever their label, have based their warrant to do all that is needful, useful, and prideful upon their claim to superior enlightenment—that is, to their special insight into the nature of men and things which purports to make the area of beneficence rendered directly proportional to the degree of power exercised. In short, all modern despots have been, in theory, enlightened despots. Their title to rule remains at least as anomalous covertly as it was overtly in the eighteenth century. Let the voter beware.

Notes

Introduction

1. Hugo Grotius, *The Law of War and Peace*, tr. Francis W. Kelsey (New York, 1925), pp. 12, 14.

2. *Hobbes's Leviathan* (Oxford, 1909), pp. 98, 121-23; Howard Warrender, *The Political Philosophy of Thomas Hobbes: His Theory of Obligation* (Oxford, 1957), pp. 322-23; Raymond Polin, *Politique et philosophie chez Thomas Hobbes* (Paris, 1953), pp. xix-xx, 223.

3. Samuel I. Mintz, *The Hunting of Leviathan: Seventeenth-Century Reactions to the Materialism and Moral Philosophy of Thomas Hobbes* (Cambridge, 1962), p. 149.

4. *The Chief Works of Benedict de Spinoza*, tr. R. H. M. Elwes (New York, 1951), 1: 201-7, 291-303.

5. Leonard Krieger, *The Politics of Discretion: Pufendorf and the Acceptance of Natural Law* (Chicago, 1965), pp. 35-36; Hans Medick, *Naturzustand und Naturgeschichte der bürgerlichen Gesellschaft* (Göttingen, 1973), p. 47.

6. Krieger, *Politics of Discretion*, pp. 160-62.

7. John Locke, *Two Treatises of Government*, ed. Peter Laslett (Cambridge, 1964), pp. 79-89; Medick, *Naturzustand und Naturgeschichte*, pp. 67-75.

8. "Distortion" is of course not used here in the pejorative sense which denotes the perversion of something from its true or natural form. It is used rather in a

more neutral sense to indicate the modification of something from its original form and meaning without acknowledgment of the change. For the historiographical application of distortion, see Leonard Krieger, "The Distortions of Political Theory: The XVIIth Century Case," *Journal of the History of Ideas* 25 (1964): 322-24, 331-32.

9. J. G. A. Pocock, *The Ancient Constitution and the Feudal Law: A Study of English Historical Thought in the Seventeenth Century* (New York, 1967), pp. 236-37.

10. "A Letter concerning Toleration," *The Works of John Locke* (London, 1823), 6: 10-13.

11. Grotius, *The Law of War and Peace*, p. 20.

12. H. R. Fox Bourne, *The Life of John Locke* (London, 1876), 2: 152-55.

13. Printed in ibid. 1: 174-94.

14. *Leviathan*, pp. 548, 556.

15. C. B. Macpherson, *The Political Theory of Possessive Individualism: Hobbes to Locke* (Oxford, 1962), pp. 13-15.

16. Locke, *Two Treatises*, p. 87.

17. Grotius, *The Law of War and Peace*, p. 12.

18. *Leviathan*, pp. 9-19.

19. Grotius, *The Law of War and Peace*, pp. 42-43.

20. "A Letter concerning Toleration," *Works of John Locke*, 6: 51.

21. Ibid., p. 34.

22. Samuel Pufendorf, *De jure naturae et gentium* (Lund, 1672).

23. Christian Thomasius, *Fundamenta juris naturae et gentium sensu communi deducta* (Halle, 1705); Christian Wolff, *Jus naturae methodo scientifica pertractatum* (Frankfurt, 1740-48).

Chapter 1

1. Roscher's first essay on the fundamental developmental forms of the state, with due place assigned to the enlightened despots in them, was admittedly a mere sketch—"Umrisse zur Naturlehre der drei Staatsformen"—which he published in the *Berliner Zeitschrift* for 1847-48. He emphasized the economic relevance of absolutism in general and enlightened absolutism in particular later in his career, when he wrote his influential *Geschichte der National-Oekonomik in Deutschland* (Munich, 1874), pp. 380-81. Finally, he made the most elaborate presentation of the whole scheme in *Politik: Geschichtliche Naturlehre der Monarchie, Aristokratie, und Demokratie*, 2d ed. (Stuttgart, 1893), pp. 250-51, 281-99 (1st ed. 1892). For Treitschke, see Heinrich von Treitschke, *Deutsche Geschichte im neunzehnten Jahrhundert*, 4th ed. (Leipzig, 1886), 1: 70 (1st ed. 1879). For Koser, see Reinhold Koser, "Die Epochen

der absoluten Monarchie in der neueren Geschichte" (1889), in *Zur preussischen und deutschen Geschichte: Aufsätze und Vorträge* (Stuttgart, 1921), pp. 332, 365 ff. For a twentieth-century version of this traditional interpretation of enlightened despotism as the "third and final stage" of "royal despotism in Europe," see Geoffrey Bruun, *The Enlightened Despots* (New York, 1929), esp. pp. 29-30. On this whole discussion see Helen Liebel, "Der aufgeklärte Absolutismus und die Gesellschafts-Krise in Deutschland im 18. Jahrhundert," in *Absolutismus* (Darmstadt, 1973), pp. 489-90.

2. For the following discussion of contemporary criticisms of the eighteenth-century idea of enlightened despotism, see Peter Gay, *The Enlightenment: An Interpretation* (New York, 1966-69), 2: 492-501; Arthur Wilson, *Diderot* (New York, 1972), p. 635; Maurice Tourneux, *Diderot et Catherine II* (Paris, 1899), p. 144; Guillaume-Thomas Raynal, *Histoire philosophique et politique des etablissements et du commerce des Européens dans les deux Indes* (Amsterdam, 1770), 6: 391; ibid. (The Hague, 1774), 7: 216-17; ibid. (Geneva, 1780), 4: 481-82; ibid. (Geneva, 1783), 9: 123-24, 10: 25-27; Helen Liebel, "Der aufgeklärte Absolutismus," in *Absolutismus*, pp. 489, 532-33 and note; Immanuel Kant, "What Is Enlightenment?" and "Perpetual Peace: A Philosophical Sketch," in Lewis White Beck, ed. and trans., *Critique of Practical Reason and Other Writings in Moral Philosophy* (Chicago, 1949), pp. 291, 315. The reference to Raynal in Fritz Hartung, "Der aufgeklärte Absolutismus," in *Historische Zeitschrift* 180 (1955): 16-17, implying his general defense of enlightened despotism, is misleading both in the text and in the note. The general political disquisition on contemporary Europe, in which Raynal's statement about the happiest of governments being the just and enlightened despot's was contained, was promised in the original edition of 1770 but was not submitted to the publisher. (See 6: 426 of the 1770 edition.) When the volume was submitted and published in a subsequent edition some four years later, the passage on enlightened despotism was in the form of a rejected opinion, as indicated in my text above.

3. See esp. Heinz Holldack, "Der Physiokratismus und die absolute Monarchie," *Historische Zeitschrift* 145 (1931): 537-45; Fritz Hartung, "Der aufgeklärte Absolutismus," ibid. 180 (1955): 40-41; Peter Gay, *Voltaire's Politics* (New York, 1959), pp. 167-71; Robert Derathé, "Les philosophes et le despotisme," in Pierre Francastel, ed., *Utopie et institutions: le pragmatisme des lumières* (Paris, 1963), pp. 73-75.

4. Georges Lefebvre, "Enlightened Despotism," in Heinz Lubasz, ed., *The Development of the Modern State* (New York, 1964), pp. 52-53; Hartung, "Der aufgeklärte Absolutismus," *HZ* 180:25. Advocates of this relationship frequently admit cases of idiosyncratic enlightened practice but deny any characteristic or representative function to them.

5. Friedrich Meinecke, *Machiavellism: The Doctrine of Raison d'Etat and Its Place in Modern History*, tr. Douglas Scott (New York, 1965), pp. 272-75, 282-83.

6. Gay, *The Enlightenment* 2:492–94.

7. Francois Bluche, *Le despotisme éclairé* (Paris, 1968), pp. 318–19, 331–34. Bluche admits "enlightened monarchy" but only in a technical administrative sense; in every other sense there were "flagrant contradictions between Enlightenment (*Lumières*) and monarchy." See also Alfred Cobban, *In Search of Humanity: The Role of the Enlightenment in Modern History* (New York, 1960), p. 161, and Fritz Hartung, "Die Epochen der absoluten Monarchie in der neueren Geschichte," *Historische Zeitschrift* 145 (1931): 48–52.

8. Holldack, "Der Physiokratismus und die absolute Monarchie," *HZ* 145: 547–49. For variations of this theme of parallel tensions, see Bluche, *Le despotisme éclairé*, esp. pp. 334–51, which resolves the "ambivalence" in the theory and practice of "enlightened monarchy" with the practical thesis of the enforced emulative development of underdeveloped societies, and Helen Liebel, "Enlightened Despotism and the Crisis of German Society," *Enlightenment Essays* 1 (1970): esp. 168, which resolves the "crisis" with the equally practical but politically reversed thesis of the conservative freeze imposed by monarchs of underdeveloped society against the pressure of development. For the intellectual "oscillations" on the theme of enlightened absolutism, both in France and in Italy, that followed from the alignment of intellectuals with the cause of reform in societies whose circumstances were only beginning to shake conservative domination, see Furio Diaz, *Filosofia e politica nel Settecento francese* (Turin, 1962), pp. 556, 563, and Franco Venturi, *Settecento riformatore* (Turin, 1969), pp. 721–24.

9. Thus: Leo Gershoy, *From Despotism to Revolution, 1763–1789* (New York, 1944); John G. Gagliardo, *Enlightened Despotism* (New York, 1967); Stuart M. Andrews, ed., *Enlightened Despotism* (London, 1967); Roger Wines, ed., *Enlightened Despotism: Reform or Reaction?* (Boston, 1967); and Liebel, "Enlightened Despotism," in *Enlightenment Essays*. Even the hypercritical Franco Venturi has not hesitated to use "enlightened despotism" repeatedly and synonymously with enlightened monarchy and enlightened absolutism: see his *Utopia and Reform in the Enlightenment* (Cambridge, 1971), pp. 8, 9, 14, 43, 70, 131, and his *Settecento riformatore*, p. 721.

10. For the use here of the malleable terms "paradigm" and "category," see note 19 below.

11. *The Political Writings of Jean Jacques Rousseau*, ed. C. E. Vaughan (New York, 1962), 2: 43.

12. "Pouvoir" and "Représentants," in Diderot, *Oeuvres politiques* (Paris, 1963), pp. 36, 40–54; Jeremy Bentham, *A Fragment on Government and An Introduction to the Principles of Morals and Legislation*, ed. Wilfrid Harrison (Oxford, 1960), pp. 94–95, 98–99; [Paul Henri Dietrich d'Holbach], *La politique naturelle* (London, 1773), 1: 72, 95–97.

13. "Despotisme," *Encyclopédie, ou Dictionnaire raisonné des sciences, des arts et des métiers* (Paris, 1751–65), vol. 4 (1754).

14. *La politique naturelle* 1:120, 152-53; *Ethocratie* (Amsterdam, 1776), p. 6.

15. Rousseau, *Political Writings* 2: 28, 46.

16. For absolutism as a model of an organically limited autocracy, conceptually distinct from despotism, see especially Hartung, "Der aufgeklärte Absolutismus," *HZ* 180:40-41, and Leonard Krieger, *Kings and Philosophers, 1689-1789* (New York, 1970), pp. 242-47. The present essay represents a revision, and presumably an advance upon, the views therein expressed. For the complementary usage of absolutism and despotism, see Derathé, "Les philosophes et le despotisme," in Francastel, ed., *Utopie et institutions*, pp. 67-68.

17. Thus: Geraint Parry, "Enlightened Government and Its Critics in Eighteenth-Century Germany," *Historical Journal* 6 (1963): 180-81; Thadd E. Hall, "Thought and Practice of Enlightened Government in French Corsica," *American Historical Review* 74 (1969): 880-905; Helen P. Liebel, *Enlightened Bureaucracy versus Enlightened Despotism in Baden, 1750-1792* (Philadelphia, 1965); Bluche, *Le despotisme éclairé* (see concluding chapter, "La monarchie éclairée).

18. As an ancillary confirmation of the systematic logicality which is a connotation of absolutism in general and of enlightened absolutism in particular, it may be noted that when Wilhelm Roscher, the most theoretical of the nineteenth-century progenitors of the tradition, articulated enlightened despotism into a doctrinal component of a developmental social philosophy he wrote in the literal terms of "enlightened absolutism" rather than of "enlightened despotism." Roscher, *Politik*, p. 251.

19. It should be noted that the distinctions made here between "paradigm," "category," and "schema" do not correspond to usage in the most influential discussions of the relevant methodological problems by Thomas Kuhn and John Pocock. Kuhn uses "paradigm" to denote an operational model whose authority was explicitly contemporaneous with the age of its historical agents, but in his standard formulation he did not go on to discuss the problems of recognition and retrospection by the historian. Pocock has acknowledged the manifold differentiations in the respective roles of the historical agents and the historian in the explication of the authoritative models which represent the patterns of thought in an age, but — perhaps because of his focus on the linguistic medium of such "controlling concepts" — he has presented these differentiations as a continuum under the blanket notion of "paradigm." My usage is intended to confirm Kuhn's limitation of "paradigm" to contemporary expression and to mark with the qualitative distinctions connoted by the terms "category" and "schema" the differences in kind between explicit, implicit, and attributable historical patterns of thinking. See Thomas S. Kuhn, *The Structure of Scientific Revolutions* (Chicago, 1962), pp. 10-11, 43; and J. G. A. Pocock, *Politics, Language, and Time* (New York, 1971), pp. 13, 32-39, 278-80.

20. The most prominent text featuring despotism as a primary political category was undoubtedly the text distinguishing monarchy fundamentally from despotism (Baron de Montesquieu, *Spirit of the Laws*, tr. Thomas Nugent [New York, 1949], bk. II, 4, 5; bk. III, 5, 7-10), but the habit of denominating as "despotism" the opposite of whatever form of lawful government was being espoused was widespread. Thus see despotism vs. representative government in Diderot (*Oeuvres politiques*, p. 47), despotic vs. free government in Helvétius (*De l'esprit*, new ed. [Paris, 1843], pp. 248-72) and Bentham (*Fragment on Government*, p. 94), "republicanism" vs. despotism in Kant ("Perpetual Peace," in Beck, ed., *Critique of Practical Reason . . . ,* pp. 314-15).

21. For summaries of the literature on the varieties of "despot," "despotic," and "despotism" from the Greeks through the eighteenth century, see especially Franco Venturi, "Oriental Despotism," *Journal of the History of Ideas* 24 (1963): 113-18, and Derathé, "Les philosophes et le despotisme," pp. 58-72.

22. The variety has been documented up to the eighteenth century by R. Koebner, "Despot and Despotism: Vicissitudes of a Political Term,"*Journal of the Warburg and Courtauld Institutes* 14 (1951): 275-302; for the eighteenth century by Albert Lortholary, *Le Mirage russe en France au XVIIIe siècle* (Paris, 1951), pp. 135-50, and Melvin Richter, "Despotism," in *Dictionary of the History of Ideas* (New York, 1973), 2:8-13:

23. Derathé, "Les philosophes et le despotisme," pp. 61-65.

24. Venturi, "Oriental Despotism," *JHI* 24: 135-39.

25. Cited in Lortholary, *Le mirage russe*, p. 138.

26. August Ludwig Schlözer, *Allgemeines StatsRecht und Statsverfassungslere* (Göttingen, 1793), p. 114.

27. Isabel F. Knight, *The Geometric Spirit: The Abbé de Condillac and the French Enlightenment* (New Haven, 1968), p. 282; Derathé, "Les philosophes et le despotisme," p. 65.

28. Thus: Jaucourt, in *Encyclopédie* 10:789; Diderot, in *Oeuvres politiques*, p. 47; Helvétius, in *De l'esprit*, pp. 255-68.

29. "Discours en Sorbonne. Premier Discours: Sur l'avantage que l'établissement du christianisme a procuré au genre humaine." *Oeuvres de Turgot*, new ed. (Paris, 1844), 2: 593; "Plan du premier discours sur l'histoire universelle," ibid. 2:639. Linguet was no philosophe but he made the same point: popular resistance to the despot's abuse of power lies in the very nature of things. Lortholary, *Le mirage russe*, p. 138.

30. Jaucourt, in *Encyclopédie* 10:792.

31. Certainly there were notable cases of explicit opposition to Pope's dictum. For the case of Hume, see Gay, *The Enlightenment* 2:451. See also Schlözer, *Allgemeines StatsRecht*, p. 115, and Immanuel Kant, "Zum ewigen Frieden," in *Sämtliche Werke* (Grossherzog Wilhelm Ernst Edition), 5:670-71. But for

the context in which Pope's general idea asserting the priority of results over forms was pervasive in the eighteenth century, see below, pp. 52-55.

32. Jaucourt, in *Encyclopédie* 10:789.

33. Cited in Lortholary, *Le mirage russe*, pp. 339, 341.

34. Johann Heinrich Gottlob von Justi, *Politische und Finanzschriften über wichtige Gegenstände der Staatskunst, der Kriegswissenschaften und des Cameral- und Finanzwesens* (Leipzig, 1764), 3:75-79, 86. For analogous requirements of "order, plan, and comprehensive system" in the administrative science of statistics, see August Ludwig von Schlözer, *Theorie der Statistik: Nebst Ideen über das Studium der Politik überhaupt* (Göttingen, 1804), p. 58.

35. Justi, *Politische und Finanzschriften* 3:86-87. For citations, see Parry, "Enlightened Government," *Historical Journal* 6:182, and Gay, *Enlightenment* 2:489.

36. "Plan du premier discours sur l'histoire universelle," in *Oeuvres de Turgot* 2:637-38; "Pensées et fragments," ibid., pp. 674-75; "Premier discours sur les avantages . . . du christianisme," ibid., p. 593.

37. Pp. 78-81.

38. "Premier discours. . ."; "Géographie politique," ibid., pp. 625-26.

39. *Oeuvres complètes d'Helvétius* (Paris, 1795), 11:176-95 and 12:141-45; [Holbach], *Ethocratie* (Amsterdam, 1776), "Avertissement" and pp. 1-2; Lortholary, *Le mirage russe*, p. 341. For a specific reference to "enlightenment policy" (*Aufklärungspolitik*) see Schlözer, *Allgemeines StatsRecht*, pp. 20-21.

40. Helvétius, *De l'esprit*, p. 249.

41. [Honoré Gabriel Riquetti Mirabeau], *Essai sur le despotisme*, 2d ed. (London, 1776), pp. 18, 25.

42. Ibid., pp. 63-69.

43. Holbach, *Ethocratie*, p. 8. Again: "It would not be necessary to limit their power; the greater their authority, the more fortunate their subjects; the more force they would have the better they could combat the inveterate abuses and evils with which nations are so often afflicted. . . . But history shows us on every page that good despots are rare and that tyrants are very common; that the wisest princes are very often replaced by monsters—in the last analysis that unlimited power corrupts the mind and heart and perverts the best disposed men." [Holbach], *La politique naturelle* (London, 1773), 2:56-57.

44. Ibid. 1:96.

45. Lortholary, *Le mirage russe*, pp. 139-44.

46. Mary P. Mack, *Jeremy Bentham: An Odyssey of Ideas, 1748-1792* (London, 1962), pp. 170-72, 362-64.

47. Bluche, *Le despotisme éclairé*, pp. 334-41; Diaz, *Filosofia e politica*, pp. 118-19, 227, 504-5, 552, 556, 563-64, 610-11, 615-16, 636-37, 641;

Venturi, *Settecento riformatore*, p. 721; idem, *Utopia and Reform*, p. 129.

Chapter 2

1. (Paris, 1950).

2. For further discussion of this problem see below, pp. 67–78.

3. Gagliardo, *Enlightened Despotism*, pp. 93–94; Robert Mauzi, *L'idée du bonheur au XVIIIe siècle* (Paris, 1960), pp. 13–14; Holldack, "Der Physiokratismus und die absolute Monarchie," *HZ* 145:529, 549. In general, the role of economists in the explicit advocacy or acknowledgment of enlightened despotism is a striking one. Besides the preeminence of Physiocrats and Cameralists in the French and German versions of enlightened despotism, it can be noted that an Italian proponent like Beccaria had joined the economic reformers with a dissertation on money before he wrote his famous work on penal law, and that Wilhelm Roscher, the historiographical founder of enlightened despotism, was, despite his writings on politics, primarily an economist.

4. [Le Mercier de la Rivière]. *L'ordre naturel et essentiel des sociétés politiques*, ed. Eduard Depitre (Paris, 1910), pp. vii, 18.

5. Johann Heinrich Gottlob von Justi, *Der Grundriss einer guten Regierung* (Frankfurt, 1759), p. 21; Albion W. Small, *The Cameralists* (Chicago, 1909), pp. 413, 415, 492; "Ueber die Liebe des Vaterlandes," Sonnenfels, *Gesammelte Schriften* (Vienna, 1785), 7:107–20; Robert A. Kann, *A Study in Austrian Intellectual History* (New York, 1960), p. 170; Gay, *Enlightenment*, 2:489.

6. This is obvious in the case of the welfare-minded Cameralists and their far-ranging recommendations for the state's "police" powers in the service of marshaling all available resources for the "common happiness"; but it holds true for Physiocrats as well, with their assignment of "economic moral instruction," "protection," and "universal administration" to the sovereign. See especially Justi's *Grundsätze der Policeywissenschaft*, ed. Johann Beckmann, 3d ed. (Göttingen, 1782), passim, and Nicolas Baudeaux, *Première introduction à la philosophie économique ou analyse des états policés*, ed. A. Dubois (Paris, 1910), pp. 160–61.

7. Even the Physiocrat most prominently associated with the advocacy of a literal "legal despotism" could define the functions of the sovereign "tutelary authority" simply as the "protection and security" of landed property. Le Mercier, *L'ordre naturel*, pp. 17–18.

8. Thomas Hobbes, *Man and the Citizen*, ed. Bernard Gert (Garden City, N.Y., 1972), pp. 171, 205.

9. *Hobbes's Leviathan*, p. 133. Hobbes's emphasis.

10. The point is clear only in the Latin edition of 1668 which uses the term *authoritas*, consistently with Hobbes's meaning. The English version of 1651

applies the term "sovereign power" to the same point in one of Hobbes's ambiguous employments of the expression. Ibid., p. 212; Thomas Hobbes, *Opera philosophica quae latine scripsit omnia* (London, 1841), 3: 202; Helmut Quaritsch, *Statt und Souveränität* (Frankfurt/M., 1970), 1: 117–18.

11. The recent emphases on the structural relevance of Hobbes's schema of sacred history to the gaps in his logic of political rights and authority, and on the structural contribution of the Aristotelian tradition in substantive ethics and in the formal architectonics of knowledge to the theoretical integrity of Hobbes's cautious, late seventeenth-century follower, Samuel Pufendorf, serve to confirm the context of homogeneous order which was the essential precondition of seventeenth-century thinking. J. G. A. Pocock, *Politics, Language, and Time*, pp. 169 ff.; Horst Denzer, *Moral philosophie und Naturrecht bei Samuel Pufendorf* (Munich, 1972), pp. 244–46.

12. Diderot, *Oeuvres politiques*, pp. 14–15, 35, 37.

13. "Essai sur les formes de gouvernement et sur le devoirs des souverains," in *Oeuvres de Frédéric le Grand* (Berlin, 1848), 9: 198–99.

14. Johann Heinrich Gottlob von Justi, *Der Grundriss einer guten Regierung*, "Vorrede" and p. 33.

15. Cited in Small, *Cameralists*, 498.

16. Holbach, *Politique naturelle*, 1: 49.

17. Michel Foucault, *The Order of Things* (New York, 1970), pp. 217–19. See esp. pp. 328 ff. for the rethinking about origins.

18. Johann Heinrich Gottlob von Justi, *Die Natur und das Wesen der Staaten, als die Grundwissenschaft der Staatskunst, der Policey, und aller Regierungswissenschaften* (Berlin, 1760), "Vorbericht," pp. 72–85; Justi, *Grundriss*, pp. 222–32.

19. Ibid., "Vorrede," p. 22.

20. Cited in Small, *Cameralists*, p. 495.

21. E.g., see Alfieri's definition of tyranny, in his *Delle tirannide* of 1777, as any kind of government in which the ruler is above the law and "can exercise his despotism over everyone with impunity," whether he be "usurper or legitimate." Victor Alfieri, *De la tyrannie*, French trans. (Paris, 1875), pp. 15, 127.

22. Cited in Knight, *Geometric Spirit*, p. 283.

23. *François Quesnay et la physiocratie*, vol. 2, *Textes annotés* (n.p. 1958), pp. 740–41; Baudeaux, *Première introduction*, pp. 110, 154.

24. Le Mercier, *L'ordre naturel*, pp. 50–155 passim.

25. For this history of authority, see Leonard Krieger, "Authority," in *Dictionary of the History of Ideas*, 1: 141–62.

26. Montesquieu, *Spirit of the Laws*, p. 151; Helvétius, *De l'homme*, in *Oeuvres complètes*, 11: 114; Holbach, *Politique naturelle*, 1: 48; Diderot, *Oeuvres politiques*, p. 55.

27. Justi, *Grundriss einer guten Regierung*, pp. 5, 51; Small, *Cameralists*, p. 455 (translation slightly revised). Justi did not always hold to this delicate distinction: in other places he tended to slip into the easy identification of the common with the collective happiness. E.g., see Justi, *Die Natur und das Wesen der Staaten*, p. 45.

28. [François Quesnay], *Physiocratie, ou Constitution naturelle du gouvernement le plus advantageux au genre humaine*, ed. Du Pont (Leyden, 1768), pp. xlviii-liv, lxx-lxxi, lxxvii-lxxix, 1, 13-15, 26-37.

29. Holbach, *Politique naturelle*, 1:49.

Chapter 3

1. For this revival, see Charles G. Stricklen, Jr., "The Philosophe's Political Mission: The Creation of an Idea, 1750-1789," *Studies on Voltaire and the Eighteenth Century* 86 (1971): esp. 167-99.

2. Justi, *Politische und Finanzschriften*, 3:74-75, 79-87; Justi, *Grundsätze der Policeywissenschaft*, pp. 329-30; Justi, *Grundriss einer guten Regierung*, pp. 131, 154; Schlözer, *Theorie der Statistik*, pp. 30-31, 59-60; Christian von Schlözer, *August Ludwig von Schlözers öffentliches und Privatleben aus Originalurkunden* (Leipzig, 1828), 1:270, 342-43, 391-92; Schlözer, *Allgemeines StatsRecht*, pp. 106, 144-45.

3. Raynal, *Histoire philosophique* (1770 ed.), 6:391; ibid. (1783 ed.) 10:21, 25-27. That Raynal's political functionalism in this respect overlay his general development toward constitutional liberalism is perceptible in the repetition of his special argument for the despotic education of primitive peoples through the later editions in which he was castigating enlightened despotism as such. See ibid. 9:123-24.

4. Kant, "What Is Enlightenment?" passim; "Idea for a Universal History," in *On History*, ed. Lewis White Beck (New York, 1963), pp. 18-26; *Streit der Fakultäten*, in *Sämtliche Werke* 1:646-47.

5. Holbach, *Ethocratie*, pp. 15-16, 274-88.

6. Cited in Holldack, "Der Physiokratismus und die absolute Monarchie," *HZ* 145:542.

7. Cesare Beccaria, *Dei delitti e della pene*, ed. Piero Calamandrei (Florence, 1950), p. 375; English translation by Henry Paolucci, *On Crimes and Punishments* (New York, 1963), p. 91. Beccaria was idiosyncratic neither in this invocation of enlightened despotism nor in his alternation of it with an appeal to public opinion. The group of Italian reformers who gathered around the journal *Il Caffe* and of whom he was a member, shared his orientation in this respect. Venturi, *Settecento riformatore*, p. 683.

8. Baudeaux, *Premier introduction à la philosophie économique*, pp. 152-59; Justi, *Grundriss einer guten Regierung*, pp. 137, 158, 184-88.

9. For the first judgment see Schlözer's *Theorie der Statistik*, p. 30; for the second, see his *Allgemeines StatsRecht*, p. 115.

10. Kant, "Zum ewigen Frieden," in *Sämtliche Werke* 5:669–71; *Streit der Fakultäten*, ibid. 1:640. Kant's emphasis.

11. Boucher d'Argis, "Constitution," *Encyclopédie*, vol. 4. Characteristically for the use of the term through most of the eighteenth century, the *Encyclopédie* listed only specific juristic (including ecclesiastico-juristic) and historical meanings—and no general political meaning—for the term. The juristic sections, written by the *Encyclopédie's* favorite legal expert, Boucher d'Argis, stressed the traditional Roman administrative senses of the term. The section on "Constitution in modern history," written by Abbé Lenglet Dufrenoy, specified only the German Empire as its locus, and although Dufrenoy acknowledged that the term could indicate the statutes pertaining to the empire as a whole as well as the actual "state of government" in its particular sovereign principalities he expressly chose to treat only this second meaning of it.

12. Jean Bodin, *Six Books of the Commonwealth*, ed. and trans. M. J. Tooley (Oxford, n.d.), pp. 208–12; Montesquieu, *Spirit of the Laws*, pp. 15–16, 28; Gay, *Voltaire's Politics*, p. 315; Martin Göhring, *Weg und Sieg der modernen Staatsidee in Frankreich* (Tübingen, 1947), p. 116; Otto Gierke, *Natural Law and the Theory of Society, 1500 to 1800*, tr. Ernest Barker (Cambridge, 1934), 1:144–46.

13. *François Quesnay et la physiocratie*, pp. 736, 738, 742.

14. "Premier Discours. Sur ... l'établissement du christianisme," *Oeuvres de Turgot* 2:593, 595.

15. Ibid. 2:593–94.

16. "Pensées et fragments," ibid. 2:675.

17. Mémoire au roi sur les municipalités, sur la hierarchie qu'on pourrait établir entre elles, et sur le service que le gouvernement en pourrait tirer" (1775), ibid. 2:503, 506, 548, 550. Turgot's progressive authoritarianism was not simply the posture of one enlightened bureaucrat. As controller general from 1774 to 1776, he was supported by a whole coterie of philosophes, who regarded him as what Diaz calls "a philosopher in power." Condorcet, the future democrat, echoed Turgot with especial fidelity in this period, advising Turgot to tell the king that under the controller general's proposed constitution "authority ... would only be the more absolute for it, and the freer to do good." Diaz, *Filosofia e politica*, pp. 631–32 and n.

18. *Oeuvres de Turgot* 2:502–3.

19. Ibid. 2:508, 547–48.

20. "Plan du premier discours sur l'histoire universelle," ibid. 2:639.

21. "Premier discours sur ... l'établissement du christianisme," ibid. 2:593.

22. Beccaria, *On Crimes and Punishments*, pp. 4, 12–13, 91.

Conclusion

1. Baudeaux, *Première introduction*, p. 152.

2. Kant, *Die Metaphysik der Sitten*, in *Sämtliche Werke* 5:440.

3. "Despotisme," *Encyclopédie*, vol. 4. Emphasis added.

4. Tourneux, *Diderot et Catherine II*, pp. 143-45; Diderot, *Oeuvres politiques*, pp. 36-37; Raynal, *Histoire philosophique* (1774 ed.), 7:216. Empasis added.

5. Mirabeau, *Essai sur le despotisme*, pp. 18, 29.

6. Alfieri, *De la tyrannie*, pp. 14, 20.

7. Ibid., pp. 166-67.

8. "Über die Liebe des Vaterlandes," in Sonnenfels, *Gesammelte Schriften* 7:114-17.

9. Quoted in Kate Silber, *Pestalozzi: The Man and His Work*, 3d ed. (New York, 1973), pp. 34, 43, 55-56.

10. For the limiting case in this characterization of mass culture — France — see Robert Darnton, "Reading, Writing, and Publishing in Eighteenth-Century France: A Case Study in the Sociology of Literature," *Daedalus*, Winter 1971, pp. 223-26.

Bibliography

To compile a complete catalog of the literature relevant to the theory of enlightened despotism, pro and con, is inappropriate here, for it would be tantamount to the composition of a bibliography for the whole of political philosophy in the seventeenth and eighteenth centuries. What follows is an alphabetical listing of the sources and commentaries which have actually been used in this essay. Accessible translations have been cited where it has not been necessary to check the original.

Sources

Alfieri, Victor. *De la tyrannie*. French translation. Paris, 1875.

Argis, Boucher d' and Dufrenoy, Abbé Lenglet. "Constitution," in *Encyclopédie, ou Dictionnaire raisonné des sciences, des arts et des métiers* (Paris, 1751-65), vol. 4 (1754).

Baudeaux, Nicolas. *Première introduction à la philosophie économique ou analyse des états policés*. Edited by A. Dubois. Paris, 1910.

Beccaria, Cesare. *Dei delitti e della pene*. Edited by Piero Calamandrei. Florence, 1950. English translation, *On Crimes and Punishments*, by Henry Paolucci. New York, 1963.

Bentham, Jeremy. *A Fragment on Government and an Introduction to the Principles of Morals and Legislation*. Edited by Wilfred Harrison. Oxford, 1960.

Bodin, Jean. *Six Books of the Commonwealth.* Edited and translated by M. J. Tooley. Oxford, n.d.

Diderot, Denis. *Oeuvres politiques.* Paris, 1963.

Frederick the Great. "Essai sur les formes de gouvernement et sur les devoirs des souverains." In *Oeuvres de Frédéric le Grand.* Berlin, 1848.

Grotius, Hugo. *The Law of War and Peace.* Translated by Francis W. Kelsey. New York, 1925.

Helvétius, Claude Adrien. *De l'esprit.* New edition. Paris, 1843.

― ― ―. *De l'homme,* in *Oeuvres complètes d'Helvétius.* Paris, 1795.

Hobbes's Leviathan. Oxford, 1909.

― ― ―. *Man and the Citizen.* Edited by Bernard Gert. Garden City, 1972.

― ― ―. *Opera philosophica quae latine scripsit omnia.* London, 1841.

[Holbach, Paul Henri Dietrich d']. *Ethocratie.* Amsterdam, 1776.

― ― ―. *La politique naturelle.* London, 1773.

Jaucourt, Louis de. "Despotisme." In *Encyclopédie,* vol. 4.

Justi, Johann Heinrich Gottlob von. *Der Grundriss einer guten Regierung.* Frankfurt, 1759.

― ― ―. *Grundsätze der Policeywissenschaft.* Edited by Johann Beckmann. 3d ed. Göttingen, 1782.

― ― ―. *Die Natur und das Wesen der Staaten, als die Grundwissenschaft der Staatskunst, der Policey, und aller Regierungswissenschaften.* Berlin, 1760.

― ― ―. *Politische und Finanzschriften über wichtige Gegenstände der Staatskunst, der Kriegswissenschaften und des Cameral- und Finanzwesens.* Leipzig, 1764.

Kant, Immanuel. "Idea for a Universal History." In *On History.* Edited by Lewis White Beck. New York, 1963.

― ― ―. *Metaphysik der Sitten.* In *Sämtliche Werke.* Grossherzog Wilhelm Ausgabe.

― ― ―. *Streit der Fakultäten.* In *Sämtliche Werke.*

― ― ―. "What Is Enlightenment?" In Lewis White Beck, ed. and tr., *Critique of Practical Reason and Other Writings in Moral Philosophy.* Chicago, 1949.

― ― ―. "Zum ewigen Frieden." In *Sämtliche Werke.* English translation, "Perpetual Peace: A Philosophical Sketch," in Beck, ed. and tr., *Critique of Practical Reason* . . .

Locke, John. "A Letter concerning Toleration." In *The Works of John Locke.* London, 1823.

― ― ―. *Two Treatises of Government.* Edited by Peter Laslett. Cambridge, 1964.

[Le Mercier de la Rivière]. *L'ordre naturel et essentiel des sociétés politiques.* Edited by Eduard Depitre. Paris, 1910.

[Mirabeau, Honoré Gabriel Riquetti]. *Essai sur le despotisme.* 2d ed. London, 1776.

Montesquieu, Baron de. *The Spirit of the Laws.* Translated by Thomas Nugent. New York, 1949.

Pufendorf, Samuel. *De jure naturae et gentium.* Lund, 1672.

[Quesnay, François]. *Physiocratie, ou Constitution naturelle du gouvernement le plus advantageux au genre humaine.* Edited by Du Pont. Leyden, 1768.

— — —. *François Quesnay et le physiocratie.* Vol. 2, *Textes annotés.* N.p., 1958.

Raynal, Guillaume-Thomas. *Histoire philosophique et politique des établissements et du commerce des Européens dans les deux Indes.* Amsterdam, 1770. The Hague, 1773-74. Geneva, 1780. Geneva, 1783.

Rousseau. *The Political Writings of Jean Jacques Rousseau.* Edited by C. E. Vaughan. New York, 1962.

Schlözer, August Ludwig. *Allgemeines StatsRecht und Statsverfassungslere.* Göttingen, 1793.

— — —. *Theorie der Statistik: Nebst Ideen über das Studium der Politik überhaupt.* Göttingen, 1804.

Schlözer, Christian von. *August Ludwig von Schlözers öffentliches und Privatleben aus Originalurkunden.* Leipzig, 1828.

Sonnenfels, Josef. "Über die Liebe des Vaterlandes." In Sonnenfels, *Gesammelte Schriften.* Vienna, 1785.

Spinoza. *The Chief Works of Benedict de Spinoza.* Translated by R. H. M. Elwes. New York, 1951.

Thomasius, Christian. *Fundamenta juris naturae et gentium sensu communi deducta.* Halle, 1705.

Turgot, A. R. J. "Discours en Sorbonne. Premier Discours: Sur l'avantage que l'établissement du christianisme a procuré au genre humaine." In *Oeuvres de Turgot.* New ed. Paris, 1844.

— — —. "Géographie politique." In *Oeuvres de Turgot.*

— — —"Mémoire au roi sur les municipalités, sur la hierarchie qu'on pourrait établir entre elles, et sur le service que le gouvernement en pourrait tirer." In *Oeuvres de Turgot.*

— — —. "Pensées et fragments." In *Oeuvres de Turgot.*

— — —. "Plan du premier discours sur l'histoire universelle." In *Oeuvres de Turgot.*

Wolff, Christian. *Jus naturae methodo scientifica pertractatum.* Frankfurt, 1740-48.

Commentaries

Anderson, M. C. *Europe in the 18th Century, 1713-1783.* London, 1961.

Andrews, Stuart M., ed. *Enlightened Despotism.* London, 1967.

Bluche, François. *Le despotisme éclairé.* Paris, 1968.

Bruun, Geoffrey. *The Enlightened Despots.* New York, 1929.

Cobban, Alfred. *In Search of Humanity: The Role of the Enlightenment in Modern History.* New York, 1960.

Darnton, Robert. "Reading, Writing, and Publishing in Eighteenth-Century France: A Case Study in the Sociology of Literature." *Daedalus,* Winter 1971.

Denzer, Horst. *Moralphilosophie und Naturrecht bei Samuel Pufendorf.* Munich, 1972.

Derathé, Robert. *Jean-Jacques Rousseau et la science politique de son temps.* Paris, 1950.

— — —. "Les philosophes et le despotisme." In Pierre Francastel, ed., *Utopie et institutions: le pragmatisme des lumières.* Paris, 1963.

Diaz, Furio. *Filosofia e politica nel Settecento francese.* Turin, 1962.

Foucault, Michel. *The Order of Things.* New York, 1970.

Fox Bourne, H. R. *The Life of John Locke.* London, 1876.

Gagliardo, John G. *Enlightened Despotism.* New York, 1967.

Gay, Peter. *The Enlightenment: An Interpretation.* New York, 1966-69.

— — —. *Voltaire's Politics.* New York, 1959.

Gershoy, Leo. *From Despotism to Revolution, 1763-1789.* New York, 1944.

Gierke, Otto. *Natural Law and the Theory of Society, 1500 to 1800.* Translated by Ernest Barker. Cambridge, 1934.

Göhring, Martin. *Weg und Sieg der modernen Staatsidee in Frankreich.* Tübingen, 1947.

Hall, Thadd E. "Thought and Practice of Enlightened Government in French Corsica." *American Historical Review* 74 (1969).

Hartung, Fritz. "Der aufgeklärte Absolutismus." *Historische Zeitschrift* 180 (1955).

— — —. "Die Epochen der absoluten Monarchie in der neueren Geschichte." *Historische Zeitschrift* 145 (1931).

Holldack, Heinz. "Der Physiokratismus und die absolute Monarchie." *Historische Zeitschrift* 145 (1931).

Kann, Robert A. *A Study in Austrian Intellectual History.* New York, 1960.

Knight, Isabel F. *The Geometric Spirit: The Abbé de Condillac and the French Enlightenment.* New Haven, 1968.

Koebner, R. "Despot and Despotism: Vicissitudes of a Political Term." *Journal of the Warburg and Courtauld Institutes* 14 (1951).

Koser, Reinhold, "Die Epochen der absoluten Monarchie in der neueren Geschichte," in *Zur preussischen und deutschen Geschichte: Aufsätze und Vorträge* (Stuttgart, 1921).

Krieger, Leonard. "Authority." In *Dictionary of the History of Ideas*. New York, 1973.

― ― ―. "The Distortions of Political Theory: The XVIIth Century Case." *Journal of the History of Ideas* 25 (1964).

― ― ―. *Kings and Philosophers, 1689-1789*. New York, 1970.

― ― ―. *The Politics of Discretion: Pufendorf and the Acceptance of Natural Law*. Chicago, 1965.

Kuhn, Thomas S. *The Structure of Scientific Revolutions*. Chicago, 1962.

Lefebvre, George. "Enlightened Despotism." In Heinz Lubasz, ed. *The Development of the Modern State*. New York, 1964.

Liebel, Helen P. *Enlightened Bureaucracy versus Enlightened Despotism in Baden, 1750-1792*. Philadelphia, 1965.

― ― ―. "Enlightened Despotism and the Crisis of German Society," *Enlightenment Essays* 1 (1970). Expanded version in German translation, "Der aufgeklärte Absolutismus und die Gesellschaftskrise in Deutschland im 18. Jahrhundert." In *Absolutismus* (Darmstadt, 1973).

Lortholary, Albert. *Le mirage russe en France au XVIIIe siècle*. Paris, 1951.

Mack, Mary P. *Jeremy Bentham: An Odyssey of Ideas, 1748-1792*. London, 1962.

Macpherson, C. B. *The Political Theory of Possessive Individualism: Hobbes to Locke*. Oxford, 1962.

Mauzi, Robert. *L'idée du bonheur au XVIIIe siècle*. Paris, 1960.

Medick, Hans. *Naturzustand und Naturgeschichte der bürgerlichen Gesellschaft*. Göttingen, 1973.

Meinecke, Friedrich. *Machiavellism: The Doctrine of Raison d'Etat and Its Place in Modern History*. Translated by Douglas Scott. New York, 1965.

Mintz, Samuel I. *The Hunting of Leviathan: Seventeenth Century Reactions to the Materialism and Moral Philosophy of Thomas Hobbes*. Cambridge, 1962.

Parry, Geraint. "Enlightened Government and Its Critics in Eighteenth-Century Germany." *Historical Journal* 6 (1963).

J. G. A. Pocock. *The Ancient Constitution and the Feudal Law: A Study of English Historical Thought in the Seventeenth Century*. New York, 1967.

― ― ―. *Politics, Language, and Time*. New York, 1971.

Polin, Raymond. *Politique et philosophie chez Thomas Hobbes*. Paris, 1953.

Quaritsch, Helmut. *Staat und Souveränität*. Frankfurt/M., 1970.

Richter, Melvin. "Despotism." In *Dictionary of the History of Ideas* (New York, 1973).

Roscher, Wilhelm. *Geschichte der National-Oekonomik in Deutschland.* Munich, 1874.

— — —. *Politik: Geschichtliche Naturlehre der Monarchie, Aristokratie, und Demokratie.* 2d ed. Stuttgart, 1893.

Silber, Kate. *Pestalozzi: The Man and His Work.* 3d ed. New York, 1973.

Small, Albion W. *The Cameralists.* Chicago, 1909.

Stricklen, Charles G. Jr. "The Philosophe's Political Mission: The Creation of an Idea, 1750-1789." In *Studies on Voltaire and the Eighteenth Century* 86 (1971).

Tourneux, Maurice. *Diderot et Catherine II.* Paris, 1899.

Treitschke, Heinrich von. *Deutsche Geschichte im neunzehnten Jahrhundert.* 4th ed. Leipzig, 1886.

Venturi, Franco. "Oriental Despotism." *Journal of the History of Ideas* 24 (1963).

— — —. *Settecento riformatore: Da Muratori a Beccaria.* Turin, 1969.

— — —. *Utopia and Reform in the Enlightenment.* Cambridge, 1971.

Warrender, Howard. *The Political Philosophy of Thomas Hobbes: His Theory of Obligation.* Oxford, 1957.

Wilson, Arthur. *Diderot.* New York, 1972.

Wines, Roger, ed. *Enlightened Despotism: Reform or Reaction?* Boston, 1967.

Index